DISPENSATIONALISM IN AMERICA

by C. Norman Kraus

DISPENSATIONALISM
in AMERICA
Its Rise and Development

JOHN KNOX PRESS
Richmond, Virginia

Library of Congress Catalog Card Number: 58-10510

TO
C. K. LEHMAN
*faithful teacher and
minister of Christ*

Acknowledgments

In the writing of this book the author is especially indebted to Dr. Lefferts A. Loetscher for his very helpful guidance in the initial research and preparation of the manuscript. A special vote of thanks goes also to Mr. Jack Goodwin, former assistant to the librarian at the Princeton Theological Seminary, for his generous help in securing materials which were difficult to obtain, and to Dr. Bruce M. Metzger for the loan of his personal bibliographical notes and books on the subject. Many others have helped in the typing and editing of the manuscript. Two of these who richly deserve a special note of thanks are Lois Pate and Mrs. Kraus.

C. Norman Kraus

Goshen College
Goshen, Indiana

Foreword

Dispensationalism, like other forms of premillennialism, teaches that Christ will return to earth and reign for a thousand years. But it differs from other forms of premillennialism in dividing up sacred history into a number of dispensations—usually seven—in each of which God deals with man on a different basis.

Dispensationalism was introduced into the United States by pastors of middle and upper middle class churches at just the moment when intellectual change on these social levels was creating near panic in the late 1870's and 1880's. Together with the more intellectual resistance offered by conservative Protestantism to evolution and Biblical criticism, dispensationalism constituted the vanguard of the modern fundamentalist movement. Fundamentalism of the more academic Calvinistic type still tries to maintain almost unchanged the relationship between Christianity and culture that was formulated in the days of the Protestant Reformation, in spite of the fact that in the intervening centuries Western culture has radically altered.

But dispensationalism follows a quite opposite strategy. Some three decades after Kierkegaard, and acting with very different presuppositions from his, American dispensationalism vigorously repudiated the idea of continuity between God and man, redemption and evolution, Christianity and society, which philosophical idealism was fostering. By its heightened supernaturalism, dispensationalism deliberately widened the gulf between Christianity and its environment, thus at once protecting its own faith and reducing the possibility of effective Christian influence on thought and society. One suspects that unless contemporary conservative Protestantism can achieve greater success in bringing up to date its inherited formulation of the relation between

7

Christianity and culture, dispensationalism, with its exasperated dismissal of the whole problem, will continue to be heard within the "neo-evangelical" or fundamentalist movement.

It is chiefly by its unusual philosophy of history that dispensationalism so effectively seals the Church off from the world. In this historically minded age dispensationalism was forced to recognize the reality of change, but would not allow within history itself any immanent power of development. The result was, as Mr. Kraus suggestively indicates in this book, a conception of dispensational compartments, each differing from the other, but with no continuous development from the one to the other. There is change, brought about by a succession of divine irruptions into history, but no true historical development either within or between the various "dispensations." The system is an exaggerated supernaturalism, with interaction between the "supernatural" and the "natural" kept to the barest minimum.

This conception of history lends itself, in a way, to a timely emphasis on "crisis." After nineteen centuries during which Christ had not returned physically to the earth how was it possible to vitalize the belief that He may now come at any moment? Dispensationalism answered by saying that the nineteen centuries of the dispensation of grace, or Church age, have been a "parenthesis" not covered by Biblical prophecy, and that this interval may end at any moment, when the clock of prophecy will resume its ticking. This idea of imminent crisis has, of course, a distinctive type of appeal. It means that the important changes now taking place in the secular world may at any moment be completely overshadowed by changes of cosmic significance introduced by the direct intervention of God Himself.

Dispensationalism pays a heavy price for compartmentalizing God's redemptive relation to man. In an un-Biblical and dangerous way it makes "law" and "grace" mutually exclusive, and thus flounders between the opposite dangers of legalism and antinomianism. It is Israel which, after the "rapture" of the Church, will become the Kingdom of God and the instrument of converting mankind.

The same pattern which thus exalts Israel as a restored national kingdom reduces the Christian Church, which classic Protestantism has always emphasized, to a mere parenthesis between Christ's first and second advents. Many parts of the New Testament, such as the Lord's Prayer and the Sermon on the Mount, are transferred from the Church to Israel. The organic character of the Church is dissolved into a collection of individuals plucked from the burning. Dispensationalism finds its unity across denominational lines in the persons of its leaders, in Bible institutes and prophetic conferences, and in an extensive literature, but not in any doctrine of the Church.

Dispensationalism's use of the Bible is interesting. Like critical Biblical theology it recognizes that not all Biblical texts can be woven into a single tapestry. But dispensationalism, not allowing any "documentary" divisions of Scripture, creates different "dispensations" into which it tries to distribute the Biblical material without internal contradictions. In other respects dispensationalism's use of the Bible is quite nonhistorical. Literal Old Testament history is often treated figuratively, while prophecy is interpreted literally. That is, both are used outside of their true historical context. But in spite of this literalistic approach to the Bible, dispensationalism—in contrast to some other branches of contemporary Fundamentalism—emphasizes the inner spiritual experience of the individual Christian. To be sure, Christian experience as conceived by the dispensationalist is quite well defined and no longer the fluid, unpredictable phenomenon that it was in the most dynamic days of American revivalism.

Mr. Kraus's book, here introduced, meets a real need. Dispensationalism is much more interesting—historically, theologically, and even philosophically—than the main body of American Christians have realized. Discussion of the movement, both from within and from without, has commonly been Biblical or dogmatic rather than historical. But dispensationalism's relations to its antecedents, and especially its reactions to the cultural forces of its time, call for more searching historical analysis than has previously been given it. Perhaps the inroad which dispensationalism has made on more conventional types of Protestant conservatism points those thus thrown on the defensive to a re-examination of the classic synthesis of the Protestant reformers and to a restudy of what should today be the relation between Christianity and the surrounding world. It is one of the merits of Mr. Kraus's admirable book that it offers a careful historical study of dispensationalism in a way that is clear and informing. He traces the inner development of the movement, distinguishing it from other forms of premillennialism, and evaluates it by historical criteria. The work should prove both interesting and stimulating.

LEFFERTS A. LOETSCHER

Princeton Theological Seminary
Princeton, New Jersey

Contents

Introduction

The period from the end of the Civil War to the opening of the twentieth century was one of development and change in America. Social, political, and economic patterns, as well as philosophical and theological thought, were in flux. The social and economic life of the nation were marked by rapid industrialization and urbanization which caused radical changes in the established social pattern. Industrial magnates intent on the acquisition of wealth exploited labor unmercifully, paying poor wages and assuming little or no responsibility for the health and general welfare of the workers. Immigrants arrived in large numbers, providing cheap labor for the expanding markets and rapidly swelling the population of the cities. Facilities to take care of this expansion, however, did not keep pace with the growing needs; and this in turn greatly accentuated the social unrest among the working classes.

In such an environment new social theories and solutions which were being introduced began to take root and grow. Some church leaders, of course, were quite ready to accept many of the innovations and looked upon them as a necessary adjustment to the new conditions. They welcomed new ideas, and were willing to revise their theology to include the new insights. Indeed, the underlying mood of the period was optimistic, as the phrase "the gay nineties" reminds us. The harsher aspects of the older Calvinism were tempered to the new climate. The somber evaluation of man's nature and his moral abilities was forsaken for the more favorable diagnosis of the mediating theology. The concept of God's immanence in nature and the processes of society, especially as it was understood in the framework of evolution, seemed to ensure the inevitability of progress. Charles H. Hopkins has described the developing theology of the period succinctly when he says concerning the church leaders of the post-Civil War years:

> Stressing the love of God rather than the more somber attributes of justice or majesty, this sentimentalized Protestantism tended to emphasize heaven and the rewards of religion while overlooking other equally historic doctrines. Divine judgment was now tempered by a romantic optimism; the basic Christian conception of crisis was smoothed over by the softer idea of progress. The sympathizing Jesus gradually replaced the Christ of Calvary.[1]

On the other hand, many men of a more conservative bent were not so ready to accept the innovations as progress. They were more inclined to label them "anarchism" and "nihilism." In their minds there was genuine cause for alarm. The new ideologies seemed to challenge and threaten both the political and religious institutions which had come to be taken for granted. The evangelists and teachers of the Bible and prophetic conference movements which flowered during this period belonged to this latter group. They only vaguely understood these incipient influences and defined them in general terms such as "atheism, pantheism, skepticism, and rationalism," but it is clear that they were aware of and disturbed by them. They felt that a sound appraisal of the real condition of their culture had to be made in the light of the social unrest and the growing rationalism and secularism which threatened the moral and spiritual fiber of society.

More specifically, there were three general theological tendencies which set the backdrop for the rise of the Bible conference movement with its development of distinct norms for interpretation of the Bible. They were (1) the tendency to minimize the distinctions between the natural and the supernatural and to find God immanent in the world, (2) the emphasis on direct, intuitive experience of God, and (3) the application of the norms of historical criticism to Biblical history in the context of an evolutionary philosophy.

Each of these emphases seemed to challenge directly or in-directly the orthodox view that the Bible is the supernaturally revealed Word of God. The tendency to minimize the qualitative difference between the natural and the supernatural inevitably suggested that there was no qualitative difference between the Bible and other religious books, thus challenging the whole con-cept of inspiration. Emphasis on intuition tended to minimize the importance of the literal message of Scripture and to remove its authority as an objective norm for human conduct. And still further, the application of evolutionary norms of development to Biblical history directly contradicted the traditional concept of revelation as an objective act of God in history independent of man's moral or spiritual development. Many conservative teach-ers and evangelists felt that all this tended to make the opinion and experience of man normative, and apparently this is what they refer to in their prophetic and Bible conferences as "ration-alism."

The unique method of interpretation and the theological sys-tem which was developed and nourished within the bosom of the Bible and prophetic conference movements has come to be known as *dispensationalism*. The tenets of this system have been ex-plained in many books and pamphlets, but probably the one source of dispensational teaching which is best known and most influential is the *Scofield Reference Bible*. Some have used the term "ultradispensationalism" to describe this movement since historic Christianity has always made dispensational divisions be-tween the Old and the New Testaments, but the term has not gained general acceptance. "Ultradispensationalism" has been used by the dispensationalists themselves to describe the doctrines of Bullinger and others who have carried the position further than they themselves care to take it. In keeping, therefore, with generally accepted usage we shall use the term dispensationalism as the descriptive title for the system of teaching embodied in the *Scofield Reference Bible*. No account has been taken of Bullin-ger's ultradispensational position because it has not received a large following.

Some scholars who disagree with dispensationalism feel that it should be called "modern dispensationalism." Philip Mauro and Alexander Reese, among others, maintain that the movement is entirely of recent origin. For example, Reese says:

> About 1830, however, a new school arose within the fold of Pre-millennialism that sought to overthrow what, since the Apostolic Age, have been considered by all pre-millennialists as established results, and to institute in their place a series of doctrines that had never been heard of before. The school I refer to is that of "The Brethren" or "Plymouth Brethren," founded by J. N. Darby.[2]

Those who hold the dispensationalist position resent the suggestion that dispensationalism is modern, although most of them admit that Darby and his co-workers extended and modified the doctrine to some extent. Since it is part of our purpose in this study to determine the modernity of the views propounded by Scofield, the term contemporary will be used to distinguish between the teachings of men who have followed the innovations of John Darby and the Plymouth Brethren and the dispensational systems that were developed prior to 1830.

By and large, the analyses and criticisms that have been made of contemporary premillennialism have assumed the identity of dispensationalism and premillennialism. While this assumption may be legitimate for the purpose of theological analysis, since the main trend of the movement in the recent past has been dispensationalistic, it is becoming increasingly clear that contemporary dispensationalism is not the only logical or historical outcome of premillennialism. Rather, it is a distinct historical phenomenon which has arisen within the fold of premillennialism. In America this development has taken place largely since the Civil War. Some premillennialists have rediscovered the historic position as it was held by men like Samuel H. Kellogg and Nathaniel West a generation ago, and have returned to it. One example of this return is George E. Ladd of Fuller Seminary, whose *Crucial Questions About the Kingdom of God* repudiates the fundamental dispensational distinction between the Kingdom and the Church. In his most recent publication, *The Blessed Hope,* Ladd explicitly appeals to the position held by Nathaniel West and other early leaders in the Bible conference movement to support his own position. In the light of this it seems best to further distinguish between the two positions within premillennialism. For this purpose the term *historic* will be used in contrast to *dispensationalistic.*

The approach of the conservative writers opposing dispensationalism, such as Philip Mauro, O. T. Allis, Floyd Hamilton, and George L. Murray, has been along dogmatic and exegetical lines. Harris Franklin Rall includes a historical survey of millennialism from the post-apostolic period to the present, but he devotes only a few pages to the history of the modern movement. Part two of his book is a penetrating analysis of premillennialism as a system of theology and philosophy of history. Little or no attempt has been made by any of these men to understand and evaluate the dispensational movement in its historical setting. Kromminga, who is a moderate historic premillennialist, traces the history of the broader doctrine of millennialism—that is, the belief that Christ will return and reign on earth for 1000 years. He attempts to show that contemporary dispensationalism is historically related to the Federal theology of Cocceius, but he does not give much attention to the history of the movement in America. William Rutgers, in his *Premillennialism in America,* is so opposed to any kind of premillennialism that it has been difficult for him to maintain an objective historical approach in his analysis, though he has some valuable and interesting insights. Ladd, in his *The Blessed Hope,* devotes a chapter to a brief sketch of the developments within American premillennial circles.

The liberal critics have been more dispassionate in their appraisal, but their criticism stems from a viewpoint so radically different from and opposed to dispensationalism that they sometimes fail to understand the basic problems with which the dispensationalists wrestled, or to appreciate the more profound insights which they had. Shirley Jackson Case, for example, is interested in the movement mainly as a sociological phenomenon, and his study is an attempt to show that apocalypticism has always been the product of an escapist mentality which will not face the realities of history in periods of social unrest. Francis McConnell, in the *Harvard Theological Review* (1919), made an analysis of the causes of premillennialism, pointing out that the cohesive element of the movement was not its logical coherence but its appeal to elemental human longings and emotional needs. He made no attempt to deal with the theological problems inherent in the controversy, but pointed out that liberal theology would have to be more realistic in its approach if it hoped to outdate the millennialists' appeal. George Ricker Berry has made a very illuminating and scholarly study of the premillennialists' method of interpreting the Old Testament prophecies; however, the alternative which he offers is far from satisfactory to many conservative theologians.

The only dispensationalist's attempt to give a historical perspective to the movement which I have discovered is that of Arnold Ehlert, entitled "A Bibliography of Dispensationalism," which was published in *Bibliotheca Sacra*. This bibliography begins with the early Church, and includes dispensational schemes of three or more dispensations which have appeared up to the present day. The schemes are arranged chronologically, and some explanative comments on the outlines are included, but no doctrinal or historical analysis of the material is attempted. There are histories of millennialism written by dispensationalists, but they do not treat the rise of dispensationalism as a distinct phenomenon. The following quotation from Lewis S. Chafer gives in brief compass the general position of the dispensationalist school concerning its own significance and relation to historic premillennialism. There is an evident attempt to link the two, both logically and historically.

> The term "Modern Dispensationalism" implies that Dispensationalism is *modern*. In the recovery of vital truth in the Reformation, dispensational distinctions, like various other doctrines, were not emphasized. The truths thus neglected in

the Reformation have since been set forth by devout Bible students. . . . The testimony, already cited, of Jonathan Edwards (1703-1758) that in his day dispensational distinctions were a living topic of theological discussion indicates the fact that these themes were dominant two hundred years ago. Similarly, a worthy and scholarly research of the Bible with dispensational distinctions in view was made during the last century in England by J. N. Darby, Charles H. Mackintosh, Wm. Kelly, F. W. Grant and others who developed what is known as the Plymouth Brethren movement. These men created an extended literature of surpassing value which is strictly Biblical and dispensational, which literature, however, has been strangely neglected by many conservative theologians.[3]

This present study is not primarily an attempt to refute dispensationalism, but rather to understand it. It is, however, only fair to say that the author finds himself in basic disagreement with its interpretation of the Biblical materials and with the answers which it offers to many questions. He is, nevertheless, keenly appreciative of the fact that it attempted to preserve the historic Christian concepts at a time when they were being sacrificed on the altars of liberalism and higher criticism. The main questions which have been kept constantly in mind throughout the discussion are, What is dispensationalism? and, Why and how has it become such a compelling force in conservative circles? In order to answer these questions, the movement must be seen in its historical context, and it is the purpose of this study to present such a historical analysis.

The year 1909 is, in a sense, a terminal point in the development of contemporary dispensationalism because it is the year of the publication of the *Scofield Reference Bible,* which represents the classic expression of the mainstream of the movement in America. Chafer's more complete treatment in his recently published *Systematic Theology* is little more than a systematic defense and expansion of Scofield. By and large, the same thing could be said for the other dispensationalist writers and teachers since Scofield.

For this reason, since this study is an attempt to examine the nature and dynamic of the dispensational movement rather than to write its complete history down to the present, I have limited the historical scope of the discussion to this date. It is my fervent hope that this may add a bit of background and light to the current discussion of the nature of the Bible and its historical content.

PART ONE

The Rise of Contemporary

DISPENSATIONALISM

1. PATTERNS FOR THE AGES

Age schemes are almost as old as the Christian Church. Many of the early church fathers suggested such plans, and though they often differ in the number of ages or dispensations they include in their plans there are some essential assumptions which they hold alike. The first of these is that there is only one basic dispensational division. This is the division between the Old Covenant and the New. Christ is the pivotal point in the history of God's dealing with men. Secondly, it was assumed, and even stoutly defended, that the Church under the New Covenant stood in organic succession to Israel under the Old Covenant, and that therefore the Old Testament Scriptures belonged to the Church, not to national Israel. They believed that explicit references to Christ, the Church, and the New Covenant were all to be found in the Old Testament prophets, and they accused the Jews of changing the Hebrew text of the Scriptures in order to get rid of these doctrines.

These emphases can be easily understood when one takes into account that during the earliest period of the Church's history the Old Testament Scriptures were accepted without question as authoritative for the Church. Paul was undoubtedly referring to the Old Testament when he reminded Timothy that he had known the Scriptures from a child. For the first two hundred years there was no clearly defined New Testament canon. In these first centuries Christianity carried on a running debate with Judaism concerning whether spiritual Israel (the Church) or physical Israel (the Jews) stood in the line of succession to Moses and the prophets. "What think ye of Christ?" was and is the cen-

tral question. In these circumstances it would have been surren-
der without battle to say, as contemporary dispensationalism
does, that the Church was a parenthesis in God's plan for Israel
—that the Old Testament and parts of the Gospels belonged to
Israel under the "Kingdom now in abeyance."

It is true that some of the early leaders taught that the Kingdom of God would be climaxed in history by the reign of Christ
on earth for one thousand years (a millennium), but it was without the "dispensational" distinctions common today. For example, Irenaeus, who is usually claimed as a champion of millennialism or chiliasm as it was called in the early Church, taught
that Christ is king now. "The kingship of all that is" has been
committed to Him. All those "who receive fellowship of His
kingdom" are "His disciples." [1] Even now "He rules over nations, and judges all men, and the kings, who now hate Him and
persecute His name, for these are His enemies. . . ." [2] These early
millennialists expected the Kingdom to be established in a fuller
sense in the coming age, but this was not a different Kingdom
than now exists. It was rather the triumph and fulfillment of the
Kingdom now in existence. This is quite different from the contemporary dispensationalist teaching that the millennial Kingdom is a fulfillment of Jewish aspirations to national political
sovereignty under the re-established throne of David, and that it
has no organic relation to the Church.

Those who hold the dispensationalist viewpoint claim that
there is direct continuity between these ancient age schemes and
contemporary dispensational outlines. However, they generally
admit that there is some difference between the two. Arnold
Ehlert, of Dallas Theological Seminary, has compiled a bibliography of these outlines dating back to the first centuries of the
Church. He comments that "1825 seems to be the logical divid-
ing-line between the old and the new dispensationalism. This is
not to forget that many of the roots of later systems are to be
found in works before that date, nor that much of the older
philosophy is carried over to the later period." [3] Many of the
outlines which Ehlert lists are repetitious and would add little
to our understanding of the contemporary movement. In fact, as

we have noted above, there is a real question how much significant theological and philosophical continuity there is between
the "old and the new dispensationalism." It will be sufficient for
our purposes to describe briefly the kinds of outlines which were
elaborated by men prior to John Nelson Darby, the acknowledged pioneer of the contemporary movement, and then to give
more careful attention to a representative selection of outlines
which have been worked out by men more or less under his influence.

The age schemes which were developed by Christian scholars
prior to the contemporary dispensationalist movement were generally historical in nature. Often they followed the simple pattern of Patriarchal, Jewish, and Christian. In rewriting Carion's
Chronicle, Philip Melanchthon followed this pattern and divided
all history into three periods of two thousands years each. His
first period covered the years from creation to the time of Abraham. He described this period as a time when men lived without the aid of a written law. The second time period lasted from
Abraham to Christ and was characterized by the reign of law.
The present era began with Christ. This one he called the cycle
of the Gospel.[4] Sometimes more elaborate arrangements were
made on the basis of typological or numerical interpretation of
certain passages of Scripture. One very common practice was to
arrange time into seven periods of one thousand years each, one
period for each day of the creation week. The seventh age, after
the analogy of the Sabbath day, was designated as an era of rest or
a millennium. Such outlines do have a structural resemblance to
the sevenfold outline of the ages as given in the *Scofield Reference Bible,* but here the comparison ends.

Significant Modern Dispensational Outlines and Their Use

In the period from 1830 to the present no one outline of the
dispensations seems to have established itself as the standard pattern, unless Scofield's outline has by this time attained to such
pre-eminence. Some thought that there were as few as five ages.

Others counted as many as ten. In general, however, there seems to be a preference for the number seven. The outlines which have been chosen are representative of the developing movement. They have been included either because of their author's importance in the movement or because the outline and explanations of the author represent an advance in some area toward the final arrangement found in the *Scofield Reference Bible*. In those cases where the author is especially significant a brief biographical note has been added. These outlines are given in an attempt to show what elements have gone into the composition of modern dispensational schemes and the purposes for which such outlines have been used.

John Nelson Darby (1800-1882)

John Nelson Darby was born in London, though he grew up and lived most of his life in Ireland. He lived during a period when the Established Church of England was at a low moral and spiritual ebb. He studied law and practiced for a short while in Ireland. After his conversion, however, the conviction grew upon him that he should abandon this profession for the ministry. He accordingly gave it up, and was ordained deacon in the Church of England in 1825. The following year he was ordained parish priest. He was a man of keen intellectual acumen, deep conviction, and untiring zeal.

Very soon after his ordination he began to entertain doubts about the claims and state of the Established Church. His first inner protest was concerning the domination of the Church by the State. He felt that the Church was little more than a political organization, and that Christ did not have the pre-eminent place in it. In this dissent he remained extremely high church and was strongly drawn toward Romanism like his contemporary John Henry Newman, who actually joined the Roman Church a few years later. He followed a strict discipline, and was very careful in the personal performance of religious formalities.

While in this state of indecision and doubt Darby had an accident which forced him to remain inactive during a long convalescence. During this period of inactivity he pondered deeply the fuller implications of his dissent. He says,

> During my solitude, conflicting thoughts increased; but much exercise of soul had the effect of causing the scriptures to gain complete ascendancy over me. I had always owned them to be the Word of God. . . . The careful reading of the *Acts* afforded me a practical picture of the early church; which made me feel deeply the contrast with its actual present state; though still, as ever beloved by God.[5]

It should be carefully noted that Darby's first and basic dissent was not on the question of eschatology, but on the doctrine of the Church. In a letter replying to James Kelly, Darby explained why he had left the Established Church. He said,

> It was that I was looking for the body of CHRIST (which was not there, but perhaps in all the parish not one converted person); and collaterally, because I believed in a divinely-appointed ministry. If Paul had come, he could not have preached (he had never been ordained); if a wicked ordained man, he had his title *and must be recognized as a minister; the truest minister of Christ unordained could not.* It was a system contrary to what I found in Scripture.[6]

When Darby left the Anglican Church, he did not unite with any of the dissenting churches because of their exclusive denominationalism. It was his intent to make a wider church unity possible through a nondenominational approach.

Darby's view of the Church centered around his doctrine of "the ruin of the Church," but his theological ideas are somewhat ambiguous because he does not clearly define what he means by the Church. He said that the Church is a "lowly, heavenly body . . . has no position on earth at all, as it was in the beginning— suffering as its Head did, unknown and well known—an unearthly witness of heavenly things on earth."[7] He also used the term "church" to apply to the existing organized church in some sense.[8] However, this ambiguity did not carry over into his practical program, which called for an essentially congregational fellowship of those who would withdraw from the existing organized church—either the Established Church of England or the dissenting bodies. When he claimed that the Church was apostate he clearly meant the organized church as he knew it; and his followers, who exerted a great influence in America, made a clear distinction between the Church, which is the true bride of Christ, and Christendom, which was their designation for organized Protestant and Catholic Christianity.

It is this concept of the Church that dominates Darby's eschatology. His outline of the dispensations adds little or nothing to the many schemes which were developed before and after his own. It was not until several years after his break with the Anglican Church in 1827 that he became specifically interested in prophecy. His interest in this subject is at least secondhandedly traceable to the Albury Conferences, out of which grew the Irvingite movement. James E. Bear says,

> Among the ladies who attended some of these Albury Conferences was the Countess Powerscourt. She was so delighted with the conferences that she established a similar series of conferences at Powerscourt House near Bray, in County Wicklow. These conferences continued till 1838 at least. Darby and many of the leading Brethren as well as Irvingites and others attended these meetings. Interestingly enough, these prophetic studies never led to "date-setting" among the Brethren, as they did among the Irvingites and others. But the "truths" of the distinctive nature of the Church and the "rapture" were discovered, which led to the development of a new complex of ideas which we today know as "Dispensationalism."[9]

Neatby, whom Bear is following, says that these meetings were presided over by the rector of the parish, the Bishop of Cashe, until 1833, "when the bishop was obliged to retire on account of the extreme anti-Church views which were openly avowed."[10] This again indicates the close connection between Darby's eschatology and his doctrine of the Church.

Darby's outline of the dispensations is set forth by Ehlert as follows:

1. (Paradisiacal state), to the flood
2. Noah
3. Abraham
4. Israel:
    a. Under the law
    b. Under the priesthood
    c. Under the kings
5. Gentiles
6. The Spirit
[7. The Millennium][11]

On this outline Ehlert makes the following note: "It is very difficult to get Darby's exact outline here, as he is not always a lucid writer." There seems to be some question as to whether the paradisiacal state is to be considered a dispensation, and in his chapter on "The Dispensation of the Kingdom of Heaven" he "does not indicate clearly whether he means to identify the Dispensation of the Kingdom of Heaven with what he elsewhere calls the Dispensation of the Spirit."[12]

Darby has this to say about the character of each dispensation:

> The detail of the history connected with these dispensations brings out many most interesting displays, both of the principles and patience of God's dealings with the evil and failure of man; and of the workings by which He formed faith on His own thus developed perfections. But the dispensations themselves all declare some leading principle or interference of God, some condition in which He has placed man, principles which in themselves are everlastingly sanctioned of God, but in the course of those dispensations placed responsibly in the hands of man for the display and discovery of what he was, and the bringing in their infallible establishment in Him to whom the glory of them all rightly belonged . . . in every instance, there was total and immediate failure as regarded man, however the patience of God might tolerate and carry on by grace the dispensation in which man has thus failed in the outset; and further, that there is no instance of the restoration of a dispensation afforded us, though there might be partial revivals of it through faith.[13]

In this brief explanation there are elements that will be recurring throughout the rest of the outlines and explanations; namely, the failure of each dispensation, and God's change in His method of dealing with man in each dispensation. It should also be noted that Darby made clear distinctions between the portions of Scripture which should be considered Jewish and those which should be considered Christian.

S. H. Cox (1793-1880)

Cox, an American, was an active leader in the Presbyterian Church and the moderator of its General Assembly in 1846. His outline is included because of a note by Ehlert that "it is significant in that it is, in outline, though not in nomenclature, the exact parallel of Dr. Scofield's system."[14] His outline can be found in the American edition of the Ante-Nicene Fathers. It is part of an explanatory note on Clement of Alexandria's threefold outline. His son, A. C. Coxe, who was general editor of the American edition, says that his father felt a system of sevens should be used, "thus honouring the system of sevens which runs through all Scripture." It was on this principle that he expanded Clement's outline in the following manner:

1. Paradise
2. Adam—"the first covenant after the fall"
3. Noah
4. Abraham
5. Moses
6. Christ
7. A *Millennial period*—"preluding the Judgment and the Everlasting Kingdom."[15]

Ehlert calls attention to the fact that this outline of the dispensations was based "on a multi-covenant foundation."[16] There are, however, other considerations that minimize somewhat the significance of the parallelism between this outline and Scofield's. The first is that the idea of seven dispensations appears to have been derived from numerical considerations rather than from "dispensational" implications. Secondly, he seems to hold to the historic premillennial view of the last judgment. It is not clear how much, if any, Cox was influenced by the Plymouth Brethren in his dispensationalism.

Henry M. Parsons (1828-1913)

Parsons was one of the charter members of the group which later came to be called the Niagara Bible Conference. He appeared regularly on the platform of the prophetic conferences and in the Niagara Bible Conferences. He was introduced to the 1878 Prophecy Conference as the pastor of a Presbyterian church in Buffalo, New York. Later he held a pastorate in Toronto, Ontario.

Fortunately for our study of developing patterns, Parsons has left us two age outlines from different periods of his own development. The first one appeared in the paper which he read at the Prophetic Conference in 1878. The second was presented to the Believers' Meeting at Niagara, Ontario, in 1885. The main difference between the two outlines lies in the more precise delineation of the ages found in the second one. Several of the "chronological divisions plainly marked in Scriptures" have become more clear to him with the passing of time.

The outline and comments which are given immediately below were taken from his paper, "The Present Age and Development of Anti-Christ," which was read at the Prophecy Conference in 1878. At this point we come to the movement and men that provided the immediate environment in which Scofield and his assistant editors were nurtured.

His outline is as follows:

1. Antediluvian Age from the casting out of Adam from the Garden to the deliverance of Noah.
2. Patriarchal Age—Noah to Israel's deliverance from bondage.
3. Mosaic (Jewish) Age—Moses to the "manifestation" of Christ.

4. Christian Age—Pentecost to the present.
5. A period or age to come called "Judaic dispensation." (This one is not given with the rest as a dispensation, but is spoken of in the following discussion.)

His explanation which accompanied the outline of the first four ages is as follows:

> We have here in order, First—the revelation of Grace, increasing in fullness and light to the end of the age. Second—The same principle of sin which destroyed the peace and life of Eden is seen in its bitter opposition—increasing in power and strength, by the side of, and among the children of God. Third—This contest increases till, to save the Divine Seed, judgment supernaturally interposes—destroying the wicked—and the ark carries over the flood the seed of the race to enter a new Age.
>
> Substantially, these principles will be found ruling through the Patriarchal and the following Mosaic age. With such accuracy do we find the history of these two ages repeating the same divine order, that we thus discover and derive the analogous order of our own age.[17]

The fact that Parsons uses the word "age" rather than "dispensation" is not entirely incidental. His outline is essentially historical in character. The argument assumes a parallel course for each succeeding age, and it is aimed squarely at postmillennialism. Nothing is made of the dispensational differences of each time period. This is an excellent example of the early use of the dispensational argument at the prophecy conferences.[18]

By 1885 he had expanded the number of ages or dispensations to eight as follows:

> 1. *Holiness.* This was an indefinite period of time during which Adam lived in the Garden of Eden in perfect righteousness.
> 2. *Antediluvian.* This age lasted for 1650 years and marked "the introduction of sin and man's condemnation, and also the revelation of the redemption plan."
> 3. The *Postdiluvian* age lasted 450 years and covers the years from Noah to Abraham.

4. The *Patriarchal* age also lasted 450 years covering the time from Abraham to Moses.

5. The *Jewish* dispensation includes the period from Moses to Christ, which he figures as 1450 years.

6. The *Christian* age is reckoned as 2,000 years beginning with Christ's ascension and ending with His second coming.

7. The *Millennial* dispensation of 1,000 years follows and ends in the final victory of Christ.

8. Age eight is also labeled *Holiness*. It is described as a return to the pristine state which existed before the fall.[19]

Immediately following his outline, with its calculations of the time involved in each period, he notes that the "chronological contents of the Bible are 7,000 years." He makes no further attempt to date the second coming of Christ, but the boldness with which he includes these figures reflects quite clearly the mood of the dispensationalist movement. It should also be noted that while Parsons still is inclined to use the word age in his outline, he defines the word dispensation in this discussion and defends its use to designate time periods.

William E. Blackstone (1841-?)

Blackstone is best known for his book, *Jesus Is Coming,* which was first published in 1878 as a ninety-five-page handbook to the study of prophecy. The book went through several editions and many printings. By 1917 well over 350,000 copies had been printed, and it had been translated into twenty-five different languages. Blackstone was a Methodist minister, and took an active part in both the prophetic conference movement and the Believers' Meeting for Bible Study. His outline parallels the one given by his friend and co-worker Henry Parsons in 1885. He does not give any acknowledgment for his outline to William Trotter, a Plymouth Brethren writer, but his teaching closely resembles the interpretation in Trotter's book, *Plain Papers on Prophetic and Other Subjects.* His outline of the "aions" is found in the 1886 edition of *Jesus Is Coming* on page 161.[20]

1. Eden, the aion of Innocence, terminating in the expulsion.

2. Antediluvian, the aion of *freedom* (conscience the only restraint), terminating in the flood and reduction of the race. . . .

3. Postdiluvian, the aion of government (man put under civil authority, Gen. 9:6), terminating in the destruction of Sodom.

4. Patriarchal, the pilgrim aion (Heb. 11:8-16), terminating in the overthrow of Pharaoh and his host in the Red Sea.

5. Mosaic, the *Israelitish* aion, terminating in the crucifixion and the destruction of Jerusalem.

6. Christian, the aion of mystery, terminating in the great tribulation, the coming of the Lord, the "Judgment of Nations," and another great reduction of the world's population.

7. Millennium, the aion of manifestation, terminating in Satan's last deception and the Judgment of the great white throne.

A chart showing the plan of the ages accompanies this outline, and he gives the following explanation to go with the chart:

> The within diagram is intended to illustrate the chronological arrangement of the dispensations and some of the principal events of Bible History.
>
> The division of time into days, months and years, is fixed by the movements of the earth and moon. The term century is not used in the Scriptures, but the next greater measure of time above the year (sabbatic year and Jubilee year) is the Greek term AION or English EON. . . ."[21]

He says further that the word "aion" indicates a measurement of time and not the material or physical world.[22] And again, "It will be noticed in the diagram that the aions are not of the same duration, but each marks a change in God's method of dealing with mankind."[23]

It is apparent that the main features of the system adapted by C. I. Scofield are found here, but prominence is still given to the idea of a time scheme. His main use of this scheme in the Prophetic Conference of 1886 is to show that this dispensation will end in the utter failure of the Church, but, in contrast to Parsons, he includes the concept of God's using different methods and giving different rewards in each dispensation. This is a clear indication that Blackstone was unquestionably a dispensationalist in the modern sense of the word.

A further word should be said concerning the significance of Blackstone's outline in the whole movement, since Scofield's scheme is almost its replica. In the first place, Blackstone associates the terms "innocence," "conscience," and "government" with the first three dispensations. Secondly, his outline stands in a close historical relation to Scofield's. There is no doubt whatever that Scofield knew and used this book, though, of course, it was not the only place where he might have met the same general outline. Virtually all of the leaders of the prophetic and Bible study movements gave the book extravagant praise, and not only used it themselves but also recommended it to others.

A. J. Frost

Frost was a Baptist pastor from Sacramento, California. He played an active part in the prophetic conference movement, appearing on the program of the conference in Chicago in 1886. The outline and discussion given here were taken from his paper which was read at that conference.

The context for his outline is the debate between the premillennialists and the postmillennialists concerning the course of the present age. He outlines the dispensations in order to show that each one has ended in utter failure, and predicts that the church age will end the same way. His dispensations are as follows:

1. Paradisiacal or Edenic
2. Antediluvian—Adam and Eve outside the gates of paradise to the deluge
3. Patriarchal—Noah and family to the bondage in Egypt
4. Mosaic—Moses to the death of Christ
5. Christian—"the dispensation of the Spirit"[24]

He does not list a sixth dispensation, but he believes in the millennium.

Speaking about the character of dispensations, he says:

> In every dispensation God is sovereign and man is free, and therefore the success or failure of a redemptive scheme is less or more contingent upon man's faithfulness and responsibility. The principles of divine government being the same in all ages, human nature being the same in all dispensations, we may derive much knowledge of the present tendency and the final outcome of this dispensation. . . . We shall not only find them analogous but identical in their underlying principles.[25]

This present dispensation, he says, will end with the great battle between Christ and the Antichrist, and the judgment of the nominal church. There is no discussion concerning the end of the millennium. The dispensational rhythm is described as "privilege, responsibility, apostasy, judgment."

It is difficult to evaluate Frost's relative emphasis on dispensational similarities and differences. He hints that each dispensation has a different "redemptive scheme," but he does not develop the idea. On the other hand, the "principles of divine government are the same in all dispensations," and this is the essential characteristic that is used for argument. His outline follows recognized historical landmarks of Biblical history; however, they are more than ages. They are, in the Darbyite sense, dispensations.

James Hall Brookes (1830-1897)

Brookes was undoubtedly the outstanding leader of the Bible conference movement from 1875 to the time of his death. Cameron says that after the death of James Inglis "Dr. Brookes became the accepted leader of a large circle of pastors, evangelists and Christian workers."[26] For years he was the chairman of the committee planning the Niagara Conference, and through his magazine, *The Truth,* he spread its witness beyond the conference grounds.

The writer of his obituary in *The Truth* says, "Dr. Brookes was a typical self-made man."[27] His father died when he was a small child, and early in life he was obliged to leave his home to work for his own living. At the age of fifteen he became a school-teacher. In 1851 he entered the junior class of Miami University, where he was graduated in 1853. During his senior year of college he also took work in the United Presbyterian Seminary. In the fall of 1853 he matriculated in Princeton Seminary, where he spent one year in study. During all this time he supported himself and paid his own way through school.

Brookes was ordained to the Presbyterian ministry in 1854. After serving two pastorates he was called to the Walnut Street Presbyterian Church, later called the Washington and Compton Avenues Presbyterian Church, where he served for thirty-three years till his death.[28] Besides his work as pastor and leader of the Bible and prophetic conference movements he was editor and publisher of *The Truth* magazine from 1875 to 1897.

A list of the corresponding editors for *The Truth* in 1897 gives a good indication of who the other leaders in the movement were. They included W. J. Erdman, W. G. Moorehead, H. M. Parsons, C. I. Scofield, and George C. Needham. The name of A. J. Gordon should be added to this list of leaders. He was the editor of his own paper, *The Watchword,* which also carried the announcements of the conferences and published reports of them. Except for C. I. Scofield, who had arrived on the scene more recently, these men were the backbone of the movement from the beginning.

Brookes did not formulate a dispensational outline of his own, but followed Professor Bayne of McGill University, who was a Plymouth Brethren dispensationalist. That he was not tied to any one outline is evident from the way in which he introduces the outline of Bayne. He says, *"For the sake of convenience,* let us divide the dispensations of Jehovah's dealings with man according to the view of Professor Bayne. . . ."[29]

Bayne's outline is as follows:

1. Eden dispensation, to the fall of Adam
2. Antediluvian dispensation, to the deluge

3. Patriarchal dispensation, to the fearful judgments upon Egypt
4. Mosaic dispensation, to the "total apostasy of God's ancient people . . . fit only to be torn to pieces by the Roman eagles"
5. Messianic dispensation, to the "open rejection of Messiah, and . . . his murder by execution upon the cross . . ."
6. Dispensation of the Holy Ghost or of the Gospel
7. Millennial dispensation[30]

Commenting on this outline, Brookes says,

> Thus do we see that in each of the five preceding dispensations, man, tried under any and all circumstances, has proved to be a wretched failure; and each has closed amid increasing tokens of human depravity and divine wrath. Why will it not be so in the sixth dispensation?[31]

Another outline—that of Clouser, which Brookes is said to have thought was the best that he had seen up to that time—is based on an explicit distinction between ages and dispensations. "In the dispensations, we read the story of God in redemption; in the ages, the ways of God in government."[32] For the sake of comparison it is given below.

AGES	DISPENSATIONS
I. Ante-diluvian, Adam to Noah	I. Conscience, 4004-1921 B.C.
II. Noah to Abraham	
III. Abraham to the exodus	
IV. Exodus to the captivity	II. Law, 1921 B.C.—A.D. 29
V. Gentile supremacy, Nebuchadnezzar to the Cross	
VI. The Cross to Coming of the Son of Man	III. Grace, from the Cross to second advent
	IV. The Great Tribulation
VII. The millennium.	V. Righteousness, 1000 years.[33]

The fact that Brookes does not develop an outline of his own cannot be taken as evidence that he was not a full-fledged dispensationalist. On the contrary, it is evident that he was under Plymouth Brethren influence at least as early as 1874, and we may presume at an even earlier date, since he shows signs of a well-developed system by that time. W. C. Bayne's outline of the dispensations which Brookes uses had been published by James Inglis in his magazine called *Waymarks in the Wilderness, and Scriptural Guide* in 1864. In 1871 Brookes himself published an article in Inglis' magazine which shows clear dispensational influence. There can be no doubt that the teaching and writing of Brookes did a great deal to make the dispensationalist interpretation the predominant one in the conference movement by 1900.

He used the dispensational argument in the usual way to prove the postmillennial position wrong, but he developed other facets of the argument, too. He held, along with most of the men in his fellowship, that the Church dispensation is "a dateless, timeless period or parenthesis, during which the Holy Ghost is gathering out from all nations the elect, who are to be the body and bride of Christ." This parenthetic character of the Church age is developed from an interpretation of the seventy weeks of Daniel, according to which he held that God does not count time for Israel when they are outside of their own land.[34] The Church is the parenthesis inserted between the sixty-ninth and seventieth weeks. It is a period of *"individual"* regeneration; it is to be distinguished from the Kingdom which is a period of regeneration of the "nations."[35] Further, he held that "it is the failure to recognize the marked difference between the two dispensations which has led to such utter confusion in reading the Scriptures, and to the wretched habit of 'spiritualizing' the plainest testimonies of the word concerning the divine purposes with respect to the Jews."[36]

From this it is clear that he uses dispensationalism as a method or norm of interpretation, and not only as a temporal framework for Biblical history.

The inclusion of a "messianic" dispensation in the age outlines was quite common, though none of the other schemes noted happens to have included it. It was in connection with the messianic age that Brookes further developed the postponement theory. He said that it was during this messianic dispensation that Jesus, as David's royal Son,

> . . . presented Himself to Israel, and was rejected. . . . The king being disowned, the kingdom was in abeyance, which is defined by Blackstone as follows: "When there is no person in existence in whom an inheritance can vest, it is said to be in *abeyance,* that is, in expectation; the law considering it as always potentially existing, and ready to vest whenever a proper owner appears." Our Lord did not relinquish His claim, nor surrender His right, but from that time (Mt. 13) He began to teach in parables and to speak of the *mysteries* of the kingdom.[37]

While Brookes recognized a break at Matthew 13, he taught that the messianic dispensation continued to the final rejection and crucifixion. From his discussion of the meaning of the "Kingdom of heaven" that follows the foregoing quotation, it seems clear that he did not think that Jesus had made a definite withdrawal of His messianic offer in order to inaugurate a new plan of action after the events recorded in Matthew 12. Here he differs with Scofield. On this point he quotes Blackstone, who says that the Kingdom was also offered to Israel by the apostles before they turned to the Gentiles. "Thus the kingdom came nigh unto the Jews, who spurned it, and while it waits . . . , God visits 'the Gentiles, to take out of them a people for His name.' "[38] Although there are some minor differences, this is the substance of Scofield's so-called "postponement theory."

Brookes used numerical interpretation and even allegory to support his dispensational theses. In an article entitled "The Kingdom in Type,"[39] published in 1878, he constructed an outline of future events with an allegorical interpretation of Jesus' ministry as recorded in Matthew 14 and following. He says in this context that the twelve baskets full which were left after Jesus had fed the five thousand, and the seven baskets full left after he had fed the four thousand, have dispensational significance. At another place he says seven is the number of "dispensational completeness or fullness." [40]

G. Campbell Morgan (1864-1945)

Morgan, of course, was not an American, but the outline from his book, *God's Methods With Man,* In Time: Past, Present and Future, which was published in 1898, has been included because of Morgan's great popularity and influence in this country. George E. Ladd [41] says that Morgan later repudiated such dispensational doctrines as the pretribulation secret rapture and the any-moment theory of Christ's coming. However that may be, at the time he wrote the above-mentioned book he assumed a thoroughgoing dispensational structure.

The dispensational norm has been applied to the interpretation of the ethical as well as the theological content of the Bible. Some of the early Plymouth Brethren, including Darby, suggested that a dispensational interpretation would provide a solution to the problem raised by the imprecatory Psalms and other ethical elements of the Old Testament that were below the New Testament standard. The concept that man's ethical responsibilities change from dispensation to dispensation evidently follows from the doctrine that God changes His methods of dealing with mankind in each dispensation. This dispensational distinction forms the basis on which many men today, who profess to believe in the literal interpretation and application of an inerrant Word of God, dismiss most of the ethical demands of Jesus found in the Gospels as well as the sub-Christian standards of the Old Testament. Much of Jesus' teaching is, allegedly, for the time of the Kingdom and does not have relevance for the situation in which Christians find themselves in this age.

Morgan's discussion is an attempt to follow through the dispensations and trace the developing methodology of God in history. In the presentation that follows, words and phrases that suggest these changing and developing methods are in italics.

It hardly needs to be said that nothing essentially new is found in Morgan's dispensational arrangement.

1. Eden. During this time man was tested. This was "an absolute necessity in the nature of the case, for man is a being with a will" (p. 20).

2. Fall of man to the flood. *Sacrifice was given* which ever pointed on to Christ's cross (p. 21). Man's *conscience* is under the blood (p. 22).

3. Flood to call of Abraham. "Blood and sacrifice still held their place, but God imposed upon man the duty of *mutual self-government*" (p. 22). At Babel "there came into human history the element of *nationality*" (p. 23).

4. Abraham to Moses. "In the call of Abraham, we find God taking one man upon the *principle of faith*. . . . God's purpose in calling Abraham was that of creating a new nation, held together by this unifying principle of faith . . ." (p. 24). "Israel, however, rebelled against God's rule, and ended in Egypt and slavery" (p. 25).

5. Moses to the Cross. This period is divided up into several periods which mark a development in God's dealings. With Moses the *theocracy* begins glorious but ends in degeneracy. With Saul *"earthly kingship"* as a method is instituted, but it, too, ends in captivity. With the captivity the "Times of the Gentiles" began. "At last God's kingly rule passed from them altogether; and the times of the Gentiles set in, with Media, Persia, Greece and Rome, in the ascendant" (p. 25-26). At Christ's coming, He announced *the Kingdom at hand,* but "His own received Him not."

6. Pentecost to the Rapture (Holy Spirit dispensation). The Holy Spirit is at work in every dispensation, but this is the dispensation of His fullness. *By the working of the Holy Spirit God is gathering out an elect remnant* (p. 59). Concerning the Holy Spirit's relation to this dispensation he says, "But when the Church shall be withdrawn from among men, the Holy Spirit will depart with it; for the Comforter, in accordance with the words of Jesus, abides with believers forever" (p. 65). This means "the Spirit of God in His dispensational fullness" will be withdrawn from the earth (p. 86). "The Spirit will be withdrawn in this one way—as a presence in the world which prevents the full outworking of evil" (pp. 181-182).

7. Millennium. "*Jesus will be King,* in as direct and positive a

sense as any ruler the world has ever known . . ." (p. 115).
"Then for the first time in the history of man righteousness
and judgment will be perfectly wedded" (p. 120).[42]

The word dispensation as used by most of the authors cited
combines two ideas. It signifies first a time period, and it is used
as a synonym of the Greek word *aion,* which is usually translated age or world. Viewed as historical periods, dispensations
display striking similarities. They all follow the same pattern or
cycle, ending in degeneracy and judgment. But dispensations are
not merely historical cycles. The word dispensation also carries
something of the meaning of the New Testament word *oikonomia,*
which means a plan, arrangement, stewardship, or dispensation.
Dispensations, then, are periods of time which can be clearly
discerned and marked off from other periods by the changing
methods which God employs in dealing with mankind. They are
stages in God's developing plan of the ages. While this is not the
place for extended comment upon this concept, it should be
noted that this is not the Biblical meaning of the word *oikonomia,*
nor are the two words, *aion* and *oikonomia,* ever confused in the
usage of the New Testament.[43]

Even a casual review of these outlines and explanations makes
it clear that the American writers were influenced by Darby.
Their outlines are essentially repetitions; at best, they are variations on a theme. The differences in the outlines grow out of
the relative emphasis placed on the definition of a dispensation
as a historical or theological concept. In each case a dispensation
is a combination of both elements, the theological superimposed
upon the historical. However, dispensationalism is basically theological rather than historical in its orientation. It is not primarily
an attempt to trace the rise and fall of political, social, or religious movements in the passage of time. It is, rather, a philosophy
of history—an attempt to interpret history according to a theological norm. Thus the differences which appear in the outlines
are not essential, but are merely individual applications of the
accepted dispensational norm. When this point is clearly recog-

nized it is immediately apparent what Darby's relation is to those who follow. He expounded the norm.

In order that we may understand how important and unique the influence of Darby and the Plymouth Brethren has been in the development of contemporary dispensationalism we must now examine more carefully who these Plymouth Brethren were and how their beliefs were introduced to America.

2. THE LEAVEN OF THE PLYMOUTH BRETHREN

In the debate which has raged about the orthodoxy of contemporary dispensational doctrine the question of its origin has inevitably been involved. How far can the claim that dispensationalism is merely a continuation of historic premillennialism be substantiated? As we have noted, the dispensationalists themselves admit that there is some difference between the two, but they feel that the modern system only makes explicit what was implicit in the earlier beliefs. Lewis Sperry Chafer and others praise the Plymouth Brethren very highly for the quality and insight of their Biblical exposition. They are happy to give Darby credit for his influence, but when it is suggested that the ideas which the Brethren popularized in America originated with Darby and his immediate associates a vigorous protest is heard. Ehlert feels that an examination of the many dispensational outlines which he has compiled will make it clear that the source of the contemporary movement is ancient and varied. But if dispensationalism is—as it most certainly is—a theology, a movement, a method of interpretation, then the admission that Darby and his colleagues colored the doctrine to a considerable extent is a significant admission. George E. Ladd says, "For all practical purposes, we may consider that this movement—for dispensationalism has had such wide influence that it must be called a movement—had its source with Darby and Kelly."[1]

In 1896 Robert Cameron, who along with a few other men in the Niagara Conference had reacted to some of the dispensational elements, blamed the movement completely on the Darbyists and said that they had introduced "a theory absolutely without a single advocate in all the history of the Church, from Polycarp down."[2] He was, however, referring to certain distinctive aspects of the system and not to any scheme of dispensations. The question, then, is not whether the Brethren have influenced the movement as it exists in America today, but how much they have influenced it, by what means this influence was exerted, and what has been the resultant synthesis.

The Leaven of Plymouth Brethrenism in America

The great period of expansion for the Plymouth Brethren movement is dated from 1832 to 1875, and it was during the first part of this period that Darby developed his views on eschatology and did most of his writing. Plymouth Brethren missionaries scattered to many countries all over the world, and a flood of books and tracts from Brethren leaders made their way to the Continent and to America. Darby himself visited Canada as early as 1859. He was back again for extended visits in 1864 and 1866. He came to the United States in 1870, 1872-1873, and in 1874.[3] During this time he visited New York, Chicago, Detroit, St. Louis, Boston, and Philadelphia.[4] Ironside says, "In the 70's many of these preachers from Scotland and the north of Ireland came to America and labored with great blessing, particularly in the province of Ontario and in nearby eastern states. Later the movement extended all over the two countries."[5] The great task of these preachers was to gather out of the professing Church the true bride of Christ. They were willing to preach in any pulpit opened to them, and many were. Because of their zeal and upright character they were often very influential. The pulpits of A. J. Gordon at the Clarendon Street Baptist Church in Boston, D. L. Moody in Chicago, and J. H. Brookes at the Walnut Street Presbyterian Church in St. Louis were open to them, and there was widespread sympathy for many of their views. Ironside says that "Dr. Brookes knew and loved many of them. His pulpit had often been opened to them. J. N. Darby, Malachi Taylor, Paul J. Loizeaux and others had preached in his church at various times."[6]

That they were highly respected is evidenced in the following testimonies. In 1897 Brookes wrote that they were "a people who are on the whole the soundest in faith, and most intelligent in the knowledge of our Lord Jesus Christ."[7] In this context, however, he criticizes them for their bickering and divisions. Ironside says of C. H. Spurgeon and A. J. Gordon that they "gladly acknowledged in their respective periodicals, that there are thousands of ministers in various 'systems' throughout Europe and America who, without the least sympathy with the peculiar 'church views' of the 'Brethren,' gratefully recognize their indebtedness to them for a better understanding and a fuller preaching of the Word of God."[8] Of Moody, Turner says, "Mr. Moody ever confessed his indebtedness to the writings of the Brethren for much help in the understanding of the Word. . . ."[9] One could continue such testimonies even unto the present day, but these will suffice to show the profound influence these men had.

The striking feature of their ministry was their simple exposition of Bible passages. They did not preach a series of sermons on different topics or hold series of evangelistic meetings as Moody did. Rather they held Bible study meetings. The ministry of Malachi Taylor, who died in 1897 and was succeeded for two years by A. C. Gaebelein, is a good example of how they worked. For a period of about twelve years he held a daily Bible study meeting in Temple Court in New York City. Darby himself gave such a series of studies in Farwell Hall at Moody's invitation. It was this method, taken no doubt from the Brethren's example, that was expanded and used so effectively by Brookes and his associates in Bible conferences all over the country.

Along with the oral teaching of the Plymouth Brethren went the written word. Books, pamphlets, magazines, and a torrent of tracts spread their doctrines in Canada and the United States. They set up printing and publishing houses of their own. Besides these, Fleming H. Revell advertised many of their books with warm endorsements. In 1886 Brookes wrote in *The Truth:* "Their books and tracts were largely circulated, bringing comfort and peace and joy to thousands of souls, quickening interest in the study of the Bible, and spreading like a wave of blessing through the church of England and other religious bodies."[10]

Early in the Brethren movement two viewpoints concerning eschatology emerged. As Darby developed his dispensational concepts he met with opposition within his own group. Benjamin Wills Newton (1805-1898) and the great textual scholar, Samuel Prideaux Tregelles (1813-1875), disagreed with his dispensational distinctions. George Müller who had joined the Plymouth Brethren in 1830 also felt, as he told Robert Cameron, that he had to make a choice between Mr. Darby and the Bible, and that he had chosen the Bible. But it was the "exclusive Brethren" under the leadership of Darby that made the initial contacts in America. Probably the two most popular writers, and the widest read by American ministers, were William Trotter and Charles Henry Mackintosh, although the writings of William Kelly and Darby also circulated widely.[11] Until about 1880 the literature of Tregelles, Newton, and George Müller had very little influence upon the Bible conference movement; and when it did become known it did not turn the tide of dispensationalism.

The witness of one of the men associated with the Niagara Bible Conference gives us a good idea of the extent to which Darby's views had permeated the thought and teaching of American ministers in the movement. After having said that Darby began distinctive teachings which were "a revolution . . . a theory absolutely without a single advocate in all the history of the Church, from Polycarp down," he continues, "*And, strange to say, the writings of Mr. Darby and the 'brethren' . . . have moulded the teachings of nearly all the recent writers on prophetic subjects.*"[12] Cameron is, of course, speaking of the writers within the premillennialist movement in America, and writes as one who is not in sympathy with Darby's views. But an examination of the movement verifies this observation made in 1896.

The reports of the prophetic conferences held in 1878 and

1886 give the clear impression that new ideas were being born. Ideas are sketchily traced but not logically developed. Words and terms are used in such a way that their implications are not immediately clear. The immediate source of these new ideas is not apparent because there is a lack of footnotes and acknowledgments. No doubt this can be accounted for partly by the probability that much of the new teaching came by word of mouth through the Bible studies which the Brethren held. But there can be little doubt concerning the source of these teachings after one has read the comparatively well-developed system of thought in writers like William Trotter, C. H. Mackintosh, and William Kelly. Much of what teachers like Blackstone have to say is the mere echo of this earlier literature. It is highly instructive to pause for a closer look at their writings.

Charles Henry Mackintosh (1820-1896) is best known by his initials, C. H. M. Mackintosh was not a precise theologian, and his writings, like many of the other works of this movement, are not a systematic development of the subject but rather are commentaries on Scripture which he entitles *Notes*. Neatby gives the following account and characterization of him:

> Mr. Mackintosh had been a schoolmaster, but he subsequently devoted himself exclusively to the ministry. He had very marked popular gifts, both as a speaker and a writer, and became by means of his *Notes* on the Pentateuch the principal interpreter between Darbyism and the Church at large. Unfortunately, he was an interpreter and nothing more. His thought was loose and unsystematic. He was profoundly unoriginal, and carried no compensating weight as an authority. In private life he was one of the most amiable of men, and is now remembered with kindness by all who knew him.[13]

At another place he says, "The real leaders of the Brethren would have called Mackintosh 'a popular man,' with a strong touch of depreciation; and their verdict would have been just."[14] This is the man who influenced Moody and America. His *Notes* on the Pentateuch were extremely popular and sold in enormous quantity, especially in the United States.[15] His *Papers on the Lord's Coming* have been in print until the present.

In *Papers on the Lord's Coming* one finds an insistence upon literalism, and a constant emphasis on the clarity of the prophetic word which is so easily comprehended that even a babe in Christ can understand it if he will take it at face value. There is evident distrust of creeds. It is apparent that he feels he is saying something which is new and not generally accepted. For example, he says:

> There is something peculiarly painful in the thought of having so frequently to come in collision with the generally received opinions of the professing church. It looks presumptuous to contradict, on so many subjects, all the great standards and creeds of Christendom. But what is one to do? . . . It is entirely a question as to the teaching and authority of holy Scripture.[16]

The major emphases of contemporary dispensationalism are all to be found in his writings. A few examples will make this evident. The Church is conceived as a clearly distinct entity existing only from Pentecost to the rapture of the saints. He says that there are shadows and types in the Old Testament which can now be recognized as foregleamings of the Church, but absolutely nothing explicit is prophesied of the Church's existence or destiny. In fact, this "mystery" was not revealed even by Christ while still on earth. The "gospel of the kingdom" and the "glorious gospel of the grace of God" as preached by Paul are not to be confused. Concerning distinctions between Israel and the Church he writes:

> Another important fact for the reader to seize is this, the church forms no part of the ways of God with Israel and the earth. The church does not belong to time, but to eternity. She is not earthly, but heavenly. She is called into existence dividing an unnoticed interval—a break or parenthesis consequent upon the cutting off of the Messiah.[17]

Mackintosh is gravely pessimistic concerning the professing church, and makes a clear distinction between "Christendom" and the "true Church." He writes:

> Christendom is dark and a dreadful anomaly. It is neither one thing nor another. It is not "the Jew or the Gentile, or

the church of God." It is a corrupt mysterious mixture, a spiritual malformation, the masterpiece of Satan, the corrupter of the truth of God and the destroyer of the souls of men, a trap, a snare, a stumbling-block, the darkest moral blot in the universe of God. It is the corruption of the very best, therefore the very worst of corruptions.[18]

He admits that there are yet a few genuine Christians in Christendom, but he feels that if they had an adequate sense of its character and doom, they would quickly withdraw.

On the schematic side he teaches the pretribulation secret rapture of the Church—that is, the true Church. The professing church, or Christendom, will be under the judgment of God during the tribulation and will be destroyed. While he does not give a dispensational scheme in his *Papers,* he presupposes Darby's general outline.

The exact dates when his and Trotter's books began to be widely read in the United States are very difficult to determine. Most of these books were not dated, and some of them were written anonymously. However, by 1878 both Mackintosh's and Trotter's books were being advertised by Fleming H. Revell with warm commendations. And if we are to judge the time of their entrance by the influence apparent in the teachings of Brookes, they had been on the market for some years.

The second edition of William Trotter's *Plain Papers on Prophetic and Other Subjects,* which became popular in the United States, was written sometime during the American Civil War. The first edition was published anonymously in England some ten years earlier.[19] In the 1886 edition of Blackstone's *Jesus Is Coming,* Revell advertises thus: "Trotter's *Plain Papers* have long been considered among the very best, if not the best, popular presentation of Prophetic Truth in print either in England or America."

One finds the same elements in Trotter that were evident in Mackintosh, but Trotter is more systematic in his development, and writes more at length. Concerning dispensational differences he says:

> And has it never occurred to you, dear Christian readers,
> that in the gradual unfolding of God's purposes, dispensations
> have run, are running, and have yet to run their course, *so
> widely different in their character, that what is simple obedi-
> ence and for the glory of God in one dispensation, may be en-
> tirely foreign to the character of another?*[20]

He feels, for example, that this furnishes the solution to the diffi-
culties in interpreting the imprecatory Psalms, Samuel's hewing
Agag into pieces, Elijah calling down fire from heaven to con-
sume his enemies, etc.

He contrasts the Church and Israel in several ways. Israel's
blessing is temporal, and will finally be fulfilled in an earthly
millennial Kingdom. The Church is never promised temporal
blessings. She is a heavenly creation, and in this world will have
only persecution and trial. Her blessings are spiritual. The sword
of judgment given to Israel in the previous dispensation has been
taken from the Church. It will be returned to Israel in the millennium. The purpose of this dispensation is to gather out those
who are "His co-heirs, who are to reign with Him in that kingdom, as His bride." [21] Universal blessings will not be brought
through the Church, but by restored Israel.

An even more significant difference is pointed out concerning God's method of dealing with mankind in the two dispensations. The blessing of the Church is not "conditional on obedience, as was that of Israel in the land; but [it is] blessing in
Christ, to which we are introduced, consequent on His accom-
plishment of all that the Father gave him to do." [22] In a footnote
on the same page he explains that we are saints, not by virtue of
obedience, but by "present manifestations" of the Father and
Son through the Holy Spirit. However, he says that "in some
sense" our future *rewards* as well as our present blessings are
conditioned on our obedience "as saints." Rewards are not to be
confused with eternal life, which is conditioned only by the election of God. This dispensational explanation is an attempt to
correct the doctrine of salvation by works which the Plymouth
Brethren felt was the working assumption of apostate Christen-

dom, Roman Catholicism being the most offensive in this respect. Their concern is, of course, well taken; but the dispensational distinctions between Israel and the Church and the attempt to divorce *rewards* and *eternal life* cannot be substantiated by a careful examination of the Old or the New Testament.

Trotter had a clearly defined doctrine of the postponement of the Kingdom. He did not, however, suggest that there was a time in Christ's ministry when He withdrew His offer of the Kingdom to the Jews, as Scofield later taught. He said that the Kingdom was offered to the Jews by the apostles after Jesus' death and resurrection, and that they would have been "nationally forgiven" if they had accepted it on the Day of Pentecost. This same teaching was developed by W. E. Blackstone, who seems generally to have followed Trotter's viewpoint. Trotter's own words on this subject are as follows:

> The doctrine of the New Testament is not the substitution of another kind of kingdom for that of which the Old Testament could not fail to awaken expectations, *but the postponement of the expected kingdom* because of Israel's unpreparedness to receive it; and the existence meanwhile of an anomalous state of things, expressed by the phrase "the mysteries of the kingdom of heaven," Christ was presented as king of Israel, . . . but Israel rejected Him. . . .[23]

He makes it explicit that the millennial Kingdom of Israel and the present Church dispensation are different in "character and form." [24]

In the chapter entitled "The Doom of Christendom" [25] he proposes to answer three questions, viz.: (1) What would it have been for Christendom to have continued in God's goodness? (2) Has it done this? (3) If not, what is the inevitable doom pronounced upon it? The first question is merely a supposition, and is not discussed as such. Emphasis falls upon the last two. The answer to the second question is "IT HAS NOT." It has failed on three counts. First, the purity of the Pauline doctrine of grace has been corrupted by an inclusion of works along with grace. He scores Rome heavily on this point, but points out that Protestants have not fully restored the doctrine either. Second, the apostolic concept of missions has been perverted by Rome, and within Protestantism this perversion has persisted in the form of an expectation of the millennium as a result of missionary activity. Third, Christendom has failed to maintain spiritual unity. But an organizational union of Christendom is not the means by which this unity will be recaptured because Christendom can no longer be identified with the true Church. Rather, all Christians must come out and be separate from the professing church and be joined in spiritual unity.

The answer to the third question is that Christendom will be cut off. The remnant, "the true Church," will be translated—as was Enoch—before judgment comes upon Christendom. Then, when those identified with Christendom have been cut off, a remnant of Jews and "many spared Gentiles" will form the population of the millennial earth, and restored Israel will do the millennial mission work.

It should be quite clear from this short discussion that all the essential elements of contemporary dispensationalism are already here in a well-developed form. It is not too much to say that there is nothing really original in the contemporary argument and discussion of the subject. Scofield is entirely correct in disclaiming originality for the point of view in the *Reference Bible.*

It is difficult to determine conclusively whether or not all the first leaders in the Bible study and prophecy movements held the premillennial position prior to the time that they were influenced by Darbyism. However, judging from the fact that the general position represented at the Prophetic Conference in 1878 was historic premillennialism, it seems probable that there was substantial premillennialist conviction prior to Brethren influence. As early as 1842, George Duffield, who was pastor of the First Presbyterian Church in Detroit, wrote *Dissertations on the Prophecies Relative to the Second Coming of Jesus Christ,* which was a stout defense of premillennialism against postmillennialism. This book was first prepared as a series of sermons for his congregation, and was published later at the request of friends. Other such defenses of premillennialism could also be cited which show no influence of Darbyism. On the other hand, Brookes' *Marana-tha,* which was in the third edition by 1874, shows clear evidence of such influence, and one may assume that he held these views some years prior to an exposition of them.

Secondly, it is difficult to say how quickly and how thoroughly dispensationalism was absorbed. This difficulty stems from two sources. First, Darbyite dispensationalism assumes a premillennial eschatology, and there are many areas in which they overlap. Often dispensationalism is only a matter of further defining and explaining tenets already held by premillennialists. Second, the terminology of the Plymouth Brethren was often accepted when there was no clear understanding of all the implications, and under the shell of dispensational phrases lay more or less undisturbed the meat of historic premillennialism.

It seems clear that the views of the Brethren were not immediately taken over *in toto* by the men most influential in the prophetic conference movement. Although there was a large area of agreement between them from the beginning on basic Scriptural doctrines such as the absolute inerrancy of the Scripture, the deity of Christ, His vicarious atonement, redemption by His blood received by faith alone, and a present and certain salvation, they could not accept the "church views" of the Brethren. By "church views" they meant, first, the sectarianism and strife which were manifested among them. But, more basically, they were not ready to break with the denominational setup of which they were a part. The Brethren taught that the existing denominations were not to be in any way identified with the true Church, and that Christians within the organized church should separate themselves from it. If they did not, they were identifying themselves with the apostasy. Men like Brookes and Gordon were committed to the denominational system, and would not follow on this point. In 1899 when Gaebelein took personal counsel about his proposed break with the Methodists in order to work on a nondenominational basis, he was discouraged by W. J. Erdman, one of the early leaders in the conference movement.

By way of contrast, Scofield encouraged him to make the break.[26]

The conflict of ideas on this point led to a certain amount of ambiguity and even open contradiction in the teachings and writings of the leaders of the Bible study movement. Darby could consistently say that the church was hopelessly apostate. These men could not, because they considered the revival of missionary activity to be a sign of renewed life and vigor *in* the Church even though they admitted that there was much spiritual and doctrinal degeneracy in some parts of it. In the papers which they read at the prophetic conferences they used the dispensational argument to show that the *world* would get worse, and that it was not the business of the Church to try to bring about a moral reform. They held that the Church's duty was to preach the gospel so that the Holy Spirit might call out the elect. To put it succinctly, they tried to adapt Darby's dispensationalism—which had *anti*denominationalism as a point of departure—to a *non*denominational or *inter*denominational philosophy. There were also other areas of disagreement, but by and large they stemmed from this central issue, or they were merely schematic and acknowledged to be peripheral.

Robert Cameron, one of the participants and teachers in the early Bible conferences, interpreted the development of the dispensational viewpoint in the Bible and prophetic conference movements as one of initial wholehearted acceptance and a later retraction. While there is some validity in this interpretation, it is undoubtedly an oversimplification. A more careful examination of the data seems to indicate that the first acceptance was somewhat superficial, and that as the movement progressed and the implications became clearer, some men continued their acceptance and modified their earlier views while others maintained their historic premillennial views and cast aside those innovations which were inconsistent with them. The division in the ranks came to the breaking point when younger men, acquainted only with dispensationalistic premillennialism, insisted on following it consistently. This division will be discussed further when we deal with the disbanding of the Niagara Bible Conference in 1901.

3. THE DISPENSATIONAL NORM

Dispensationalists claim above all to be Biblicists. They are quite confident that their teachings are evident even on the surface of the Scripture. Indeed, the system is so closely identified with the Bible itself that some of its adherents tend to judge the orthodoxy of other Christians by their acceptance or rejection of the system. Lewis Sperry Chafer found it difficult to understand why the significant teaching of Darby and his associates had not gained more general acceptance among conservative Christian scholars. Chafer himself is the first to have written a systematic theology in which dispensational distinctions have been employed as the unique structural and interpretative principle. For him dispensationalism is the norm for theology. He works on the assumption that his dispensational framework is identical with the Biblical structure and that the message of the Bible, therefore, cannot be properly understood unless it is viewed dispensationally. This assumption is open to question. Can dispensationalism be described as simply Biblicism? Or is the system itself a compound of theological concepts, partly Biblical, which has been used to further interpret the Scriptures? How much has it been read into Scripture and how much out of Scripture? What are the theological emphases which undergird the system?

Dispensationalism and Calvinism

Dispensationalism has never identified itself with any one theological system. However, its scheme of dispensations and emphasis on the covenants are suggestive of the teachings of John Cocceius (1603-1669), the Dutch theologian who was a leading advocate of the "federal theology." Kromminga feels strongly that the two systems are somehow historically related. Cocceius taught that God had initiated two covenants with mankind. The first was a covenant of *works* which He made with Adam. But Adam transgressed this covenant and thus incapacitated himself and all his posterity for living under it, so God made a new covenant of *grace* with mankind. Under this new covenant, which has been in force since the fall of Adam, God inaugurated the method of salvation by faith. Cocceius taught further that the covenant of grace has been administered under three economies or dispensations. He called the era of the patriarchs the "ante-legal" economy. In this period the law was given through conscience. In the "legal" era which followed it, the grace of God was administered to national Israel through sacrifices, ceremonies, and the prophets. In the Christian or "post-legal" dispensation Christ has come and God's Kingdom has been universalized. All of these dispensations, however, are administered under the covenant of grace.

There are several features of Cocceius' theology besides his schematic arrangement of dispensations which appear to be similar to contemporary dispensationalism. His theology was Biblically oriented in contrast to the more rational, systematic approach of his contemporaries. He made constant use of typology— a feature quite common in the writings and speeches of the leaders of the Bible and prophetic conferences. He conceived of an economy or dispensation in much the same way as modern dispensationalists.

But in spite of these similarities there are more essential dissimilarities which make one wary of a too facile identification of the two systems. In contrast to Cocceius, contemporary dispensationalism holds that many covenants have been given since the fall of Adam. The covenant of grace is only one of these, and it, like most of the other covenants, inaugurates a particular dispensation. One fails to find here the clear decisive teaching that the covenant of grace is "one and the same under various dispensations" as the Westminster Confession so admirably states it.[1] Further, Cocceius held that the Church and the universalizing of the Kingdom in this dispensation is the climax in God's economies. For contemporary dispensationalism it is not so, and this is a crucial difference. George E. Ladd's comment that the theology of Cocceius "is not quite the same as the doctrine now under discussion" [2] puts it aptly.

There are, to be sure, important elements of seventeenth-century Calvinism in contemporary dispensationalism, but these elements have been blended with doctrinal emphases from other sources to form a distinct system which in many respects is quite foreign to classical Calvinism. It is probably not going too far to call the dispensationalist system eclectic. For example, its emphasis upon the necessity of a personal experience with Christ, which results in assurance of salvation and in verbal testimony and praise, is akin to Pietism and reflects the influence of revivalism. And certainly its doctrine of the Church is much nearer to the sectarian than to the Reformed tradition. This eclecticism can be accounted for partially by the fact that most of the men who helped to shape the system in America were not trained theologians. As a matter of fact they distrusted theologians, even the most conservative ones, and gloried in their own simplicity and Biblicism.

Taking all this into account, it must still be pointed out that the basic theological affinities of dispensationalism are Calvinistic. The large majority of the men involved in the Bible and prophetic conference movements subscribed to Calvinistic creeds. In 1888 Samuel H. Kellogg, professor of Systematic Theology at Western Seminary, made an analysis of the theological positions of the men who signed the call to the Prophetic Conference of 1878, and concluded:

> From these figures it appears that fifty-six percent of the signers to the call were adherents either of the Westminster or Heidelberg Standards, or of the Thirty-nine Articles of the Church of England; to which must be added twenty-two per-

cent from the Baptists, known to be strongly Calvinistic; making seventy-eight percent of the total number, who are known to hold to an Augustinian theology. But to these we should probably add also the ten Congregationalists, which will make the proportion of Augustinians in the whole to be eighty-eight percent. The significance of this is emphasized by the contrasted fact that the Methodists, although one of the largest denominations of Christians in the country, were represented by only six names. . . . Such facts can hardly be accidental.[3]

A similar analysis of the smaller group of men who issued the call to the conference in 1886 reveals about the same proportions. Out of the twenty-eight speakers at the conference, including George Needham, the secretary, fourteen were either Baptist or Presbyterian, and of the rest seven belonged to churches of the Calvinist persuasion.

More direct evidence of the theological position of the group can be seen in the statement of doctrine drawn up by the committee in charge of the Believers' Meeting in 1878.[4] In this statement the verbal inspiration and inerrancy of the Scriptures, the fall and total depravity of man, and the necessity of the new birth receive heavy emphasis. Other articles state belief in the trinity of the Godhead, the personality of the Holy Spirit, the possibility of the assurance of salvation, the necessity of a holy walk, the interdenominational unity of the Church, and a premillennial eschatology.[5]

While the presuppositions of this statement are clearly those of orthodox Calvinism, yet its emphases reflect the theological influence and tendencies of its time. In common with the new theological position which was advanced by Bushnell and his successors, this statement—and the dispensationalist movement in general—expresses definite reaction against scholastic theology, and places emphasis on the possibility of assurance in Christian experience. No doubt this similarity of emphasis is due mainly to the resurgence of revivalism, which determined the mood of both theological positions. It is reflected in the ministry of men like Moody and Beecher, whose doctrinal positions were quite differ-

ent in other respects, and in the ministry of many of the most influential leaders in the dispensational movement.

Basic Theological Assumptions

The distinctive theological emphases of dispensationalism
were developed in a climate of pessimism and reaction. Darby
himself, as we have seen, was reacting strongly against the state of
affairs in the Anglican Church. In America the mood was similar, but less intense at the outset. The first Believers' Meeting for
Bible Study took on the character of a spiritual revival, and in
subsequent meetings the inroads of rationalist theology as well
as the spiritual lethargy of the churches was a recurring theme.
Some teachers said explicitly that premillennialism was a bulwark
against rationalist theology. Thus it is not surprising to find that
the theological elements which became normative in dispensationalism ran directly counter to the developing emphasis of the
"New Theology." This is already evident in the doctrinal statement of 1878 which stressed a rigid theory of verbal and plenary
inspiration, the absolute depravity of man and his helplessness
to assist in his own salvation, and the sovereign transcendence of
the triune God. These are the three tenets which became normative for the dispensationalist system, and we must take a closer
look at them.

The last of these three, the sovereign transcendence of God,
is the foundational assumption which underlies the very concept
of a dispensation. A dispensation is begun when God projects
Himself into the historical process and initiates a covenant of
His own making with some part of the human race. It ends when
He intervenes in judgment because of man's disobedience. While
there is a pattern of historical development within the dispensation, no covenant is in any way conditioned by historical processes, nor is it necessarily historically related to the covenants
which precede or follow it. The promises enumerated in the covenants are in the last analysis unconditional, because although
man cannot and does not co-operate with God, He fulfills His

promises which He sware unto the fathers. He works out His predestined purpose *in* history, but quite apart from it—and one might almost say in spite of it. Each dispensation is set off as a distinct period of time which has little or no organically historical relation to what precedes or follows. Further, God's sovereignty is exercised in the predestination and election of nations and men to a special relationship to Himself. The whole justification for giving the Jews the dominant place in God's future plan is worked out on the ground of their national election. What Israel wishes or does is quite aside from the point. God has chosen them to be His people, so they are His people come what may. The same rigid predestination is applied in this dispensation to the individual believers who have been elected to salvation. Their election is absolutely effective. Working on this assumption, contemporary dispensationalists have elaborated an almost mechanistic theory of eternal security, and have interpreted the New Testament strictly within the framework of this norm. Interpreting the Christian experience within this predestinarian framework, they make a distinction between the Christian's "standing" before God (justification), which is the result of God's sovereign predestination, and the "state" of his sanctification, which is at least in part dependent upon man's response. This distinction is so clear-cut that it makes any meaningful relation between the two impossible. In his book, *He That Is Spiritual,* Chafer says:

> By various terms the Bible teaches that there are two classes of Christians: those who "abide in Christ," and those who "abide not"; those who are "walking in the light," and those who "walk in darkness"; those who "walk by the Spirit," and those who "walk as men"; those who "walk in newness of life," and those who "walk after the flesh"; . . . those who are "spiritual" and those who are "carnal"; those who are "filled with the Spirit," and those who are not. All this has to do with the quality of daily life of saved people, and is in no way a contrast between the saved and the unsaved.[6]

Eschatologically, God's sovereign predestination is clearly the norm. This becomes clear when it is seen that each dispensation

is set off as a distinct period of time which has no organic historical relation to what precedes or follows. Thus the course and
character of any given dispensation are defined by classifying
Scripture dispensationally, and then using the relevant materials
which have been thus defined to delineate its distinguishing features. Accordingly, the sole purpose of God in this dispensation
is to gather out from among the Jews and Gentiles an "elect
bride," the Church. This group sustains a relationship to God
which He in His own sovereign grace has determined—a relationship different in *character* from that of saints in the other
dispensations.

The second doctrine which received heavy emphasis in the
system was the total depravity of man. In the words of the doctrinal statement drawn up in 1878, they believed that man is "essentially and unchangeably bad and incapable by any educa-
tional process whatever of subjection to His law." This provided
the theological justification for their pessimism. They saw that
beneath the gilt of the "gilded age" man was the same as always
—the corrupter of all the good gifts of God. Man in his sin and
inveterate rebellion is a constant factor in every dispensation. It
makes little difference what method God employs; the result is
always the same. The new chance given in each dispensation is
for the purpose of demonstrating to man his utter depravity and
inability on the one hand, and the sovereign grace of God on the
other. In such a situation, moral evolution was considered outside
the realm of possibility. In 1897 when evolutionists were beginning to link man to some ancestor antecedent to both the anthro-
poid apes and mankind, Brookes wrote:

> At a large Ministerial Association a Rev. Dr. Lyle read a
> paper defending evolution, and saying that "no one of any
> note now holds that man is descended from a gorilla. Man was
> the descendant of a lost ancestor, of a branch long since de-
> parted." Just so . . . why do not these "scholars" and "scien-
> tists" refer to another animal more intimately associated with
> men in the Bible—the ass?[7]

Many examples of this pessimism could be cited. It was a favorite theme. The two that follow point up its basically religious

quality. In 1886 A. J. Frost wrote a paper for the Prophecy Conference held that year. In it he said:

> Suppose the world improve, as it certainly will outwardly in science, art, education, discovery, invention, commerce, and in certain worldly reforms; he is short-sighted, indeed, who does not see how superficial and deceitful is all such progress, how stimulating to all human pride, and therefore exalting human wisdom, whereas it is the wisdom of God that the world by wisdom shall not know God. And it is a fact of history that religious decline is the inevitable prelude to national ruin. Science, art, literature, jurisprudence have not the power to make a state strong if its religion is corrupt, its morals base and God ignored.[8]

Speaking at the same Prophecy Conference, A. T. Pierson waxed even more flamboyant in his rhetoric.

> What is the real character of our present civilization? We may as well face the facts. It is gigantic in invention, discovery, enterprise, achievement; but it is gigantically worldly; sometimes and somewheres [sic] monstrously God-denying and God-defying. This "Christian civilization" has produced giants in these days, men of renown, but they often use their intellect, knowledge, and fame only to break down, as with the iron flail of Talus, all Christian faith. Philosophy now blooms into a refined and poetic pantheism or a gross, blank materialism or a subtle rationalism or an absurd agnosticism. Science constructs its systems of evolution and leaves out a personal God; spontaneous generation becomes the only creator, natural law the only determining power, and natural selection the only Providence.[9]

The dispensationalist movement has been severely criticized at this point. It has been charged with cutting the nerve of Christian activity and labeled with "ostrich tactics," "escapism," and "obstructionist to moral progress." In fairness to the movement, several things need to be pointed out that are often overlooked. In the first place these men were not defeatists. Their pessimism was more akin to what would be called realism today. They despaired of man and man's efforts to effect any basic moral or spiritual progress. They did not despair of God's grace. They sought to face the facts, and events since their day have justified their candor. Secondly, their pessimism did not produce inactivity. Celebrated missionaries such as Hudson Taylor belonged to their ranks, and congregations representative of this movement have been among the most ardent supporters of the Church's mission program. These things have been often overlooked because the critics themselves begin with a more or less naturalistic bias which defines Christian activity in social terms. To such critics much of their activity seemed irrelevant and ineffective. On the other hand, it is very clear that in their reaction against an optimistic social program proposed as the means of Christianizing society, dispensationalists have made the very inexcusable mistake of almost completely neglecting to work out the social implications of the Gospel. They have tended to promote a pietistic type of religious experience which displays zeal and emotion at rally meetings, but is not intelligently related to what is often termed the "secular" vocations of life.

Finally, the dispensationalists put forward a strict, mechanical theory of verbal inspiration as a bulwark against the inroads of Biblical criticism. They were convinced that the critics were actually infidels working on naturalistic assumptions, and that to accept any of their insights would amount to denying the unique, supernatural character of the Bible. Though they may not have worded it this way, the immediate problem to which they addressed themselves was the relation of the message of the Bible and the act of revelation itself. Is the Bible a communication of supernaturally revealed knowledge? Are its very words the words of God? They answered these questions in the affirmative with a great show of confidence because they believed that any answer short of a resounding yes would detract from the infallibility and hence the authority of the Bible. They recognized clearly that revelation was by orthodox definition supernatural, and by supernatural they meant qualitatively distinct from the natural order. They set an impassable gulf between the inspiration of genius and the inspiration of the Holy Spirit. This, of course, is also true of the contemporary movement.

In a different context one might suspect that their emphasis on the qualitative difference between the natural and supernatural could have led them to welcome Bushnell's insight concerning the inability of human language to express absolute (supernatural) truth, and hence the necessity for its intuitional perception. But it was quite the opposite. The supernatural was considered a priori to be rational according to the highest natural standards, and it was defended purely on rational grounds. Thus the Bible, being the Word of God, was a priori perfect from start to finish in every sentence, word, and syllable according to the highest standards of human reason. To suggest that there might be one flaw in any of the information given to us in its pages would have been equal to suggesting that it was not the Word of God. From such a canon it logically follows that the revelation in Genesis is just as perfect in every respect as the revelation given hundreds of years later in the New Testament, which is precisely what these men believed.

The first article of the statement of faith drawn up by the leaders of the Believers' Meeting for Bible Study clearly states their theory of inspiration.

> We believe "that all scripture is given by inspiration of God," by which we understand the whole of the book called THE BIBLE; nor do we take the statement in the sense in which it is sometimes foolishly said that works of human genius are inspired, but in the sense that the Holy Ghost gave the very words of the sacred writings to holy men of old; and that His divine inspiration is not in different degrees, but extends equally and fully to all parts of these writings, historical, poetical, doctrinal, and prophetical, and to the smallest word, and inflection of a word, provided such word is found in the original manuscripts. . .[10]

While they were only vaguely acquainted with the more technical aspects of Biblical criticism, they sensed that the orthodox definition of revelation was in danger of being undermined if the norms of evolution were applied to the development of revelation in the Old Testament. Yet they seem to have been influenced enough, perhaps unconsciously, by the thought of their time to recognize the validity and force of the new genetic view of history which lay back of the attempts to formulate a philosophy of historical development in terms of evolutionary change. They also believed in "progressive revelation." But at this point they were involved in a conflict if not a dilemma. How could they reconcile their belief in a perfect, infallible revelation with the idea of progress? Progress suggests development from that which is less than perfect toward that which is perfect. But each revelation of knowledge is a perfect whole in itself. Therefore to speak of progressive revelation would seem to be a contradiction of terms.

Now the early spokesmen for dispensationalism did not spell out the problem in these terms. But it is clear that they thought of their system as an apology for orthodox theology, and it seems impossible to understand the dynamic and true significance of the movement unless we see it in its contemporary theological context. Accordingly, dispensationalism can best be understood as an attempt to define progressive revelation at a time when the concept of organic historical development was beginning to be applied to the history recorded in the Bible. Because they believed that the concepts of immanence and evolution undercut the orthodox doctrine of a supernatural revelation, the dispensationalists sought a rationale of Biblical history which would preserve its theological relationships as they had been explained in the orthodox tradition of Calvinism.

Whether it is possible to do justice to the idea of progress and development in revelation when one begins with the premise of dispensationalism that every part of the Bible is in itself a perfect inerrant revelation is quite another matter. The dispensationalists themselves attempted to escape the dilemma by defining progress in terms of a graded series of tests which God has applied to man. What emerges is a concept of historically independent dispensations based on a series of perfect revelations which are to govern man's conduct during a given period of time. These revelations are progressive only in the sense that each new one presupposes the knowledge of those which have preceded it. There is progression, but no progress in the histori-cal sense. The inspiring concept of *Heilsgeschichte,* or holy his-tory, which begins with the first glow of revelation to the fathers and progresses into the blazing splendor of Christ, the Word made flesh, is utterly lacking.

PART II

The Relation of
DISPENSATIONALISM
to
PREMILLENNIALISM

4. THE BELIEVERS' MEETING FOR BIBLE STUDY

Dispensationalist scholars show little historical self-awareness. This is evident in their facile identification of their own position with the millennialism of the early Church. In their histories of millennialism they give little or no consideration to the special genius of their own position. It is, I think, more than coincidental that while a modern dispensationalist scholar has gone to great pains to collect a bibliography of dispensationalism—organized, to be sure, in chronological order—no attempt has been made to write a definitive history of the movement. This same naïveté characterizes their approach to the Bible. It never seems to have occurred to the teachers and evangelists of the Bible conference movement that they were reading the Bible from a different historical perspective than Irenaeus, or even Jonathan Edwards. They identify Biblicism and dispensationalism. Claiming to find dispensationalism on the surface of Scripture solely through direct Bible study, they are inclined to see only superficial differences between premillennialism and dispensationalism, and they question seriously whether anyone can be a premillennialist without being a dispensationalist. For example, Chafer says:

> A new claim has been recently made by some, namely, "I am a Premillennialist, but not a Dispensationalist." This statement evidently supposes that Premillennialism is a belief in an event which is isolated from all that precedes and all that follows it. . . . In reality Premillennialism becomes a dominating feature of interpretation, since it bears on the whole divine program from its beginning to its end. As well might it be argued that though the sun rises in the morning it will neither

be preceded by darkness nor accompanied by light as to con-
tend that Christ will come to the earth again, as the Scriptures
relate that coming to all that precedes it and all that follows,
without causing the most stupendous dispensational changes.[1]

This statement suggests that dispensationalism is necessarily
the logical outcome of premillennialism. The theological aspects
of this assumption have long been debated pro and con, and it is
not our purpose to repeat them here. What is proposed in the
present chapter is an analysis of the historical relationship of the
two doctrines as they developed in the Bible and prophetic conference movements.

Although premillennialism existed in America before dispensationalism, it became vocal and aggressive in its dispensational
form through the Bible and prophetic conferences. Dispensationalism had already been introduced prior to the first Believers'
Meeting, and because of this one cannot trace a clear development from historic to dispensational premillennialism in the literature of the movement. This does not mean that there is no
development. There clearly is, but one must look below the surface to detect it. There are several clues by which the development can be traced. For example, the uses made of dispensational
arguments change perceptibly. Then there are the points of difference between historic and dispensational premillennialism
which become manifest within the movement as positions are
more clearly defined. Finally, one senses an increasingly articulate
reaction of the group to the forces about them, and an increasing
emphasis on the dispensational system as a canon of orthodoxy.

The Rise of the Believers'
Meeting for Bible Study

What has come to be known as the Niagara Bible Conference
began in 1876 when a group of ministers and evangelists met for
a private period of Bible study. Because of the success of the first
meeting and the interest manifested by the local community, they
decided to hold such a meeting the following year, adopting the

name Believers' Meeting for Bible Study for their organization. These Bible study meetings should be distinguished from the prophetic conferences which have been held periodically since 1878.[2] The Believers' Meeting was conducted as an institute for general Bible study. The prophecy conferences were limited for the most part to the discussion of prophetic subjects, and were, in fact, large rallies where papers were read and addresses were given. They were an outgrowth of the Believers' Meeting for Bible Study, and the same personnel served in both types of meetings.

The purpose of the Believers' Meeting was direct study of the Bible itself. However one might estimate or criticize the interpretations of the teachers in this movement, the sincerity of their attempt to make the Bible central and normative is above question. E. P. Goodwin, pastor of a Congregational church in Chicago, voiced the basic conviction of the whole group when he said:

> The only question for us is, what do these authorities— these books of God's revealed will teach? . . . The chief difficulty in all discussions upon Scripture doctrines lies in my judgment in this, that the authority of Scripture is not made supreme. So long as men insist upon squaring belief to the canons of philosophy, or science, and demand that everything shall approve itself before the bar of their reason, so long there can be no certainty in the things of faith. . . . I assume the absolute, infallible authority of this book as the word of God.[3]

For them the Bible was above all the "perfect" book. As J. D. Herr put it, "The book is a grand mosaic, divinely perfect in all its parts, and perfect in its divine completeness."[4] Its message is the same from beginning to end. God is the one author; the words are His words. Every part is in complete harmony with every other part. These claims, which were shared by all their conservative brethren, were interpreted by them to mean that the language of Scripture is uniform in its usage—that every type, every symbol, every word, whether in Hebrew, Aramaic, or Greek, has essentially the same meaning in every place it is used.

G. Campbell Morgan said that the "symbolism of Scripture, with regard to color, numbers, figures of speech, in every case displays the closest harmony."[5]

It was further maintained that the major theme of the Bible is prophecy. Indeed, prophecy in its apocalyptic form represents the pinnacle of revelation! G. S. Bishop explained that

> the real evolution of our human nature is presented in the book of Daniel, supplemented by St. John's revelation, *the one book being the flower and consummation of the Old Testament as the other is of the New.*
>
> For, as revelation in the Old Testament begins with theophanies, or direct appearances of God, followed by prophecy or a subjective communication, and *ending in Apocalypse, the objective, where the veil is swept away* . . . so is it in the New Testament, where we have first the manifestation of God in the flesh in the gospel; then New Testament prophecy in the Acts and Epistles, and finally, the ravished Seer of Patmos companioned by angels, outside of all earthly horizons.[6]

The assumption that followed hard on this thesis was that the prophetic word is completely understandable. There could be no doubt of its meaning if it were only admitted that language means literally what it says. Henry Lummis stated this explicitly at one of the prophecy conferences. He declared:

> I do not admit the affirmation [that prophecies are difficult to understand]. I insist that the New Testament statements conform to the laws of language as truly as do those of Xenophon. And the predictions of Jesus are as easy to be understood, even before their fulfillment, as are the utterances of Peter in his sermon on the day of Pentecost, or the words of Paul when he addressed the Athenians on Mars Hill.[7]

They described their methodology as "grammatico-historical." Speaking for premillennialism, Kellogg explained what this meant.

> Whether their conclusions be right or wrong, their arguments evidently depend on the rigid application of the grammatico-historical, inductive method of interpretation, which

Bengel in the last century did so much to introduce, and which, it is not too much to say, has secured the adhesion of the chief part of the most eminent exegetes of our day. Premillennialists, therefore, are everywhere marked by the most emphatic rejection and repudiation alike of the allegorical, the dogmatic, and the so-called rational systems of interpretation, as also of the eschatological conclusions which the application of one or other of these methods has led men to adopt.[8]

This statement was subscribed to *in toto* by the dispensationalists, though it was interpreted in a literal and mechanical way which would not have been satisfactory to all historic premillennialists. For most of the pastors in America who leaned toward dispensationalism this meant in practice a grammatical examination of the words of the English translation, and an acceptance of their literal meaning. Their concept of history was so colored by dispensationalism that this really amounted to a grammatico-dispensational interpretation of the Scripture. Indeed they admitted quite freely that dispensational norms should be applied to it in order for it to yield its true meaning. In doing this they were seemingly unaware that they themselves were applying dogmatic norms of the strictest sort to their interpretation.

These then were the assumptions and methodology with which these men approached the Scripture as the infallible source of truth. However, the final secret of their confidence in this quest lies not in their methodology, but in their belief that they as sincere followers of Christ were being led into truth by the Holy Spirit. J. D. Herr, a Baptist minister from New York, noted that since the Bible is the infallible Word of God "it requires an infallible interpreter," and that such an interpreter had been given in the person of the Holy Spirit. He continues:

> No matter how intelligent and scholarly the student of prophecy may be, he will be wholly unfit to comprehend the mind of God in relation to the future unless he assumes the proper attitude of a devout inquirer after truth. Scholarship may understand the written word, but only the man taught and indwelt by the Holy Spirit can properly grasp the incarnate word. . . .[9]

This assumption, which is shared by evangelical Christians of all schools, was combined with the preceding assumptions and interpreted by these men in such a way as to suggest that other men who did not share their beliefs were disqualified to interpret Scripture. It discouraged sound critical scholarship, and cut its adherents off from the thinking of other men who were working on the same problems. In a word, the movement was self-contained and self-sufficient.

According to A. C. Gaebelein, the Believers' Meeting of 1876 was the result of an earlier private meeting of six men held near Chicago during the previous summer. Four of the six were Nathaniel West, James H. Brookes, W. J. Erdman, and H. M. Parsons.[10] W. J. Erdman also mentioned the 1875 meeting in his announcement of the meeting in 1879,[11] but Brookes made no reference to it when he outlined the beginnings of the movement in 1878. He speaks of the meeting in 1876 as the first one.

In 1876 the men mentioned above, along with A. J. Gordon and others, met at Swampscott, Massachusetts, for fellowship and Bible study. Writing in 1878, J. H. Brookes outlined briefly how and why these Believers' Meetings for Bible Study came into being. The account is significant enough to be quoted in full.

> In July, 1876, a few brethren, having peculiar love for each other, and precious fellowship in the truth, agreed to spend a little season together in a retired spot on the sea coast. They were either pastors or evangelists, and after a year of incessant toil, they were glad to hear the voice of the Master saying, "Come ye yourselves apart into a desert place, and rest awhile." (Mark vi. 31). It was their wish to be alone with Him, and hence they carefully avoided any public notice of the time and place of meeting. But they were soon led to exclaim with His bride, "Thy name is as ointment poured forth," (Song of Sol. i. 3); and like the disciples in the days of His flesh, they found that "He could not be hid," (Mark vii. 24).
>
> Many who resided in the vicinity received the richest spiritual blessings, that in some instances at least were imparted in manifested power to the churches with which they were connected. Several hours each day for a week were passed in the

prayerful study of God's word; and all of these hours proved to be times of refreshing from the presence of the Lord. So abundant and manifold were the tokens of His approval and favor, the brethren could not doubt they had been gathered together by the Holy Ghost unto His name alone. They therefore determined before their separation to assemble the following year under the title and designation of the "Believers' Meeting for Bible Study."

In July, 1877, they convened at Watkins' Glen, New York, and again the power of the Lord was present in a marvelous way to heal and to strengthen. None who had the privilege of attending the entire course of Bible study for a week can ever forget the solemn and thrilling revelations that were made by the Holy Spirit of the glory of Christ's person, the value of His finished work for believing sinners, and the preciousness of His wondrous word. To many it was like the scene on the Mount of Transfiguration, a gleam of millennial beauty, a foretaste of millennial joy, leading them to exclaim with Peter, "Lord, it is good for us to be here," (Matt. xvii. 4).

In the last week of June, 1878, the brethren assembled at Clifton Springs, New York upon the kind invitation of Dr. Henry Foster, who entertained several of them as his guests. He renewed the invitation to assemble at the same place and time next year, and it was resolved to accept it, if the Lord will.[12]

Annual reports of these conferences were published in the magazines edited by Brookes and Gordon. Often the reports of the earlier meetings are in abbreviated or condensed form, but they give a picture of the general pattern and content of the meetings. The Swampscott conference is typical of those which followed. The meeting extended through seven days, and "the time devoted to study was crowded with expositions, illustrations, and explanatory remarks."[13] Five different topics were studied during the week. They were "Person and Work of the Holy Spirit," "Holiness or Sanctification," "How to Study the Bible," "What and How to Preach," and "The Second Coming of Christ."[14] Daily class sessions were held on each of these subjects throughout the week. From the nature of the report, the method of procedure seems to have been to trace the different aspects of each subject through the Bible, and discuss interpretations. The only textbook was the Bible.

The conference at Watkins Glen, New York, in 1877 is praised as a great "exhibition of the unity of the Spirit and of the fellowship of saints."[15] But things were not so smooth in the meeting at Clifton Springs, New York, the following year. Brookes mentions that some who had no sympathy with the objects of the meeting stirred up controversy, but he does not say what the areas of disagreement were. He merely says, "Controversy hereafter will not be allowed under any circumstances."[16] His comment, "many suppose that this [the Second Coming] is the only topic discussed and some have circulated the report that we have fixed the day, or at least the year, of our Lord's return," suggests that this may have been the point argued. In order to avoid such controversy Brookes made it clear in his announcements of the meetings that they were not interested in soliciting a large attendance. Only those sincerely interested in spiritual renewal and refreshment were welcome.

Because of the brevity of these early reports, and because they deal only with the formal discussions, it is difficult to determine just how much emphasis was given to the discussion of "dispensational truths." There are, however, indications from the first that it was a live issue. In 1876 a note is made that H. M. Parsons was unable to attend for the first few days, and that "the interval was occupied with readings on 'Dispensational Truth,' and kindred subjects, the notes of which were not preserved."[17] In the same report one finds other indications of its presence. For example, in his topic, "Person and Work of the Holy Spirit," Brown discussed "when the Dispensation of the Spirit began and when it will end. . . ." J. H. Brookes taught a pretribulation, secret rapture. He echoed the language of C. H. Mackintosh when he said, "In this coming [the rapture] the unbelieving world feels no interest, and hence *the shout of our descending Lord may not be heard by uncircumcised* ears. . . ."[18] In the report of the 1877 conference it is noted that "The coming of the Lord in its bearing upon Israel, the Church, and the world at large, received much attention, and of course it was found to be a most profitable subject for study and meditation."[19] Brookes said, however, that there was "not a shadow of truth" in the idea that the second coming of Christ was the only topic discussed.[20]

On the surface of James H. Brookes' account it appears that the Believers' Meeting arose merely out of a desire on the part of a few pastors for spiritual recreation and fellowship. There are indications, however, that there was more at stake than recreational fellowship. In the first place, it is interesting to note that the meetings were patterned after the Bible study meetings which Darby had held at various churches throughout the United States and Canada. The topics for discussion also show this new influence. When we recall that Darby himself had been in the States for an extended ministry in the years immediately preceding the rise of the Bible conference movement, and, further, that he had ministered in the pulpits of the very men who gave the initial impetus to the movement, there can be little room for doubt that Darby and other early Plymouth Brethren preachers gave direct stimulus and at least indirect guidance to the movement. The ideas which they introduced called for a reinterpretation of some aspects of traditional conservative theology, and it appears that the men who had begun to absorb the new doctrines were seeking the consultation and fellowship of kindred spirits in a common exploration.

Another evidence that there was more at stake than recreational fellowship is found in the preamble of the theological statement which they drew up near the beginning of the movement. They explained that it was necessary to state the basis upon which they could extend their fellowship because:

> So many in these latter times have departed from the faith, giving heed to seducing spirits, and doctrines of devils; so many have turned away their ears from the truth, and turned unto fables; so many are busily engaged in scattering broadcast the seeds of fatal error, directly affecting the honor of our Lord and the destiny of the soul . . .[21]

The statement itself, as we have noted earlier, continues in the same mood, and many of its articles explicitly contradict concepts which were gaining acceptance in academic and theological circles. While it would be incorrect to read all of the later reactionary mood back into this beginning, it is quite clear that we have here a principal root of the fundamentalist movement which was to reach its flaming climax some fifty years later. All this seems to indicate that the Believers' Meeting was also an attempt, consciously or unconsciously, to form a line of defense against the new thought which was beginning to offer formidable opposition to conservative theology.

However we account for their rise, the Bible conferences were an immediate and overwhelming success. Almost from the beginning the men in charge began to receive requests to set up similar meetings in other localities. These requests came from groups both in Canada and in the United States. W. J. Erdman, who was secretary for the Believers' Meeting, was delegated by the group to go ahead with this work of expansion, and under his leadership the movement became widespread. In the late 1890's and early 1900's still other meetings were set up with no direct relation to the original Believers' Meeting, which in the meantime had taken the name Niagara Bible Conference. Arno C. Gaebelein, of whom we shall hear more later, was active in promoting these later conferences.

5. THE FIRST INTERNATIONAL PROPHECY CONFERENCES

Enthusiasm for the new teaching on prophetic subjects was running high among both laity and clergy. The Bible conference movement had caught the imagination of many earnest lay Christians from among many denominations. The time was ripe for the advocates of premillennialism to seize the offensive. And seize it they did! Following the example of their fellow believers in England they opened an all-out campaign by sponsoring an international prophecy conference. The leadership for such a conference naturally fell to the men who were prominent in the Bible conference movement. James H. Brookes himself apparently acted as chairman of the "self-constituted" committee which issued the call for the conference, and in his report of the conference he says that Major D. W. Whittle, a popular evangelist and Bible teacher, was chosen as secretary.[1] Gaebelein says that the idea for such a conference was suggested by Nathaniel West (1824?-1906), a Presbyterian minister and scholar from Cincinnati, Ohio.[2] West had formerly been a professor in the Presbyterian seminary at Danville, Kentucky, and played an important role in the prophetic and Bible conference movements. He served as the conference secretary in 1878 and was editor of the published report entitled *Premillennial Essays of the Prophetic Conference.*

The prophetic conferences, following the example of the Believers' Meeting, were designedly interdenominational. For example, the men on the committee which issued the call for the first conference represented at least six denominations: Presbyterian, Episcopal (U.S.), Reformed Episcopal, Baptist, Dutch Re-

formed, and Anglican (Canada). Besides these, the men who endorsed the "Call for the Conference" represented further the
Methodists, Congregationalists, Adventists, United Presbyterians,
and Lutherans. There were also several names with no denominational specifications. Essentially the same was true of the conference held in 1886.

The Conference of 1878

The first International Prophecy Conference held in the
United States convened on October 30, 1878, in New York City in
the Church of the Holy Trinity, a Protestant Episcopal congregation. The reason for holding such a conference was stated in the
"Call for the Conference" which had been published in sympa-
thetic magazines. The opening paragraph of this call puts it quite
succinctly.

> When from any cause some vital doctrine of God's Word
> has fallen into neglect or suffered contradiction and reproach,
> it becomes the serious duty of those who hold it, not only
> strongly and constantly to re-affirm it, but to seek by all means
> in their power to bring back the Lord's people to its appre-
> hension and acceptance. The precious doctrine of Christ's sec-
> ond personal appearing has, we are constrained to believe,
> long lain under such neglect and misapprehension.[3]

The conference program was made up of a "series of carefully prepared papers on the pre-Millennial advent of the Lord
Jesus Christ and connected truths."[4] In each case the reading of
these papers was followed by open discussion. Besides these
written essays a number of "addresses" were given, most of which
were not published in the report of the conference.[5] It might be
noted in this connection that the publication resulting from this
conference is by all odds the most scholarly and restrained of the
conference publications to 1918. It rated a review in the *Bibliotheca Sacra,* which was not a dispensationalist publication at that
time, and other scholarly journals show awareness of the conference in articles published shortly afterward.

At the end of the conference five resolutions were passed which show the general theological orientation of the conference. The resolutions affirm (1) the absolute authority of Scripture, (2) the literal fulfillment of Old and New Testament prophecy, (3) the imminency of the second coming of Christ, (4) the progress of evil during this age, and (5) the duty of the Church to pray, watch, and work.[6]

In analyzing the elements of dispensationalism present in the papers read at the conference it is necessary to remember that the main thrust of the conference was toward establishing the premillennial advent. Therefore, the unity of the group against a common opponent, postmillennialism, was stressed. Most of the dispensational teaching or terminology used in the conference was only incidental to the main theme. This in itself, however, is interesting and significant in light of the fact that the next conference, held eight years later, shows a more integrated combination of the two interpretations.

The most striking example of full-fledged dispensationalism at this 1878 conference is found in the closing speech given by W. P. Mackay. The tenor of the whole speech is explicitly dispensational. Even the figurative interpretation of I Chronicles 12:39, which provides the Biblical context for his speech, is suggestive of William Kelly's dispensational exposition of the Gospel of Matthew. He testified concerning his own experience:

> Before, through God's grace, I saw these blessed truths, my reading of Scripture was "considerably mixed up." Awkward texts, ever and anon, would come up, for which I could make no place. . . . Thus it is with much of our ordinary eschatology. Text after text is found for which there is no place. Entire dispensations are lost sight of. Jewish truth gets hopelessly mixed up with Gentile truth, and the Church's hope gets sadly crushed out by both.[7]

He defined the work of the Church and the Christian's attitude toward government according to the dispensationalist norm. He said that the Church has been making a "serious mistake . . . for want of this intelligence" on this point. "Instead of gathering out a people for the Lord, the Church has been trying to gather all the people. Instead of going with the drag-net through all the sea, the Church has been attempting . . .to catch all the fish in a few favorite pools." Also, "as to the government of this world we are to have intelligence." Mankind "has tried every form of government and failed," but the Christians with dispensational understanding "are calm through all, and wait for a King to reign in righteousness."[8]

All this might be taken as good evidence for the early assimilation of dispensationalism among American premillennialists except for the fact that Mackay was a visitor to the conference from Hull, England.

As far as dispensational outlines are concerned, only one was elaborated. R. W. Clark alludes to another one, however, in an excerpt from G. F. C. Fronmuller's interpretation of I Corinthians 10:11 in Lange's Commentary. He quotes:

> It is to be noticed that the return of Christ shall be preceded not only by several ages, but also by several ends of ages, with typical final judgments, as St. Paul speaks of τὰ τέλη τῶν αἰώνων. The flood, the dispersion of the ten tribes, the judgment of Judah, but especially the destruction of Jerusalem and the conquest of Palestine, were in a certain sense such final judgments.[9]

The scheme is not basic to the line of thought, and is not discussed further.

The only dispensational outline given in the report is found in Henry M. Parsons' paper, "The Present Age and Development of Anti-Christ."[10] His essay is an attempt to demonstrate from the Bible that the future of this age will bring religious and moral decadence rather than a millennium. It will produce not Christ, but Antichrist. His dispensationalism is a part, in fact the first part, of this demonstration. He argues that all the ages before have ended in decay, judgment, and deliverance of the faithful remnant by an act of God, and that this clear pattern of the "same divine order" in the preceding ages is indicative of what we may expect in the present age. The assumption underlying this argument is the similarity and continuity of the ages. No artificial differences in the dispensations are urged upon us in order to set out the character and limits of the period. The dispensations are, as a matter of fact, chronological divisions. Thus the word "age," which the author himself uses, is the correct one. These are not dispensations as technically defined by the dispensationalists themselves.

But the use or non-use of an outline of dispensations or ages is not the most important criterion. The real impact of dispensationalism upon the men at this conference can be judged better by examining their definitions of the Church and the Kingdom and their relation to each other. Historic premillennialism made a clear, sharp distinction between the two, in contrast to postmillennialism which more closely identified them. The difference between historic and dispensationalist premillennialism on this point does not lie in the careful distinction made between the Church and the Kingdom as two separate distinct parts of God's plan for history. Rather, it lies in the dispensationalist's attempt to associate the Kingdom entirely with the Jews, and to make a qualitative distinction between the two dispensations. Nor can belief in the restoration of the Jews and the literal fulfillment of the material blessings promised by the Old Testament prophets be pointed to as evidence of dispensational influence. Many of the men of the conference shared the belief that the Jews would be restored to their own land and would in the end be converted. The distinctly dispensational addition to this doctrine was that the new covenant made with the restored Israel in the Kingdom was not to be identified with the covenant which Christ made with the Church.

Speaking to this last point, Bishop W. R. Nicholson, who explicitly states his firm belief in both the restoration of the Jews and the literal fulfillment of the material blessings as a result of Israel's conversion, said in his paper, "The Gathering of Israel":

> The spiritual blessings of millennial Israel will be the same as are ours now. They will be sons of God (Hosea 1:10); so are all Christians now. They will be under the mediator-

ship—sacrifice and priesthood—of the New Covenant (Jer. 31:31; Heb. 8:6); so are we. They will please God, and therefore must have been brought into living union with Christ, through the Spirit, even as we, for "they that are in the flesh (unregenerate) can not please God." (Rom. 8:8).[11]

In much the same way C. K. Imbrie emphasizes the essential continuity between the two dispensations. In his paper, "The Regeneration," he says:

> Let it be remembered, that it is according to this very same new covenant, as the writer of the Epistle to the Hebrews tells us, not only Israel, in his day of return, but all of us, have forgiveness and salvation—the new covenant in Christ. Could words declare more plainly that, under this new covenant, the nation, as a nation, is to be delivered from its iniquities. . .?[12]

This is in contrast to the present-day insistence that a different covenant—Jewish in character, and closely associated with the Davidic covenant—will be instituted with the restored Jewish nation. Further on in the same essay Imbrie says, "The church of God in every age is one; and her hope so far as it is revealed, in every age is the same. Why should the church, in our age, be deluded . . . ?"[13] That this statement is made as a part of an argument for the literal fulfillment of Old Testament prophecy in the millennium in no way minimizes its value as evidence for the lack of dispensational distinctions.

Imbrie further describes the millennial age as a step forward in the "regeneration" of the earth, which will be completed at the close of the millennium with "the destruction last of all of death, and then the establishment on the earth of the redeemed forever."[14] It is a period more glorious than now—the world renovated by fire, nations serving the Lord—but only leading to the time when all enemies having been destroyed, the Kingdom is complete and becomes eternal.

The relation of the Kingdom and the Church was discussed by Professor Henry Lummis, a Methodist from Monson, Massachusetts. We would, therefore, naturally expect to find the most clear-cut discussion of the distinctions between the Kingdom and the Church in his essay. He says, "I say, then, that no more absolute separation of kingdom and church could be made, without labored effort, than is already made in the New Testament by the terms employed in representing each."[15] He contrasts assemblies of believers or denominations, the churches (plural), with the Kingdom (singular). "The kingdom is everlasting, the church temporary." Yet the Kingdom is not to be merely identified with heaven as the everlasting home of the saints. It will come "on earth." All this is in contrast to the view that the Church includes the patriarchs and righteous of the old dispensation as well as the new and is the Kingdom already established—in other words, postmillennialism. The Church is a distinct, new creation which began on the day of Pentecost. He says that "if the Kingdom be in the world at all, it must be subjectively rather than objectively—in a spiritual rather than a literal sense."[16]

The question which is of special interest to us is whether or not this is an example of contemporary dispensationalism. The indications are that it is not. The thrust of the article is against the postmillennialists' identification of the Church and Kingdom as one continuous manifestation of the work of God from the beginning. It represents the more distinct break between the Old and New Testaments which the premillennial position assumes, but it is very interesting to note that this "absolute separation of kingdom and church" is really more chronological than qualitative. The basic argument is linguistic and not dispensational. The specific differences between the Church and Kingdom are not made clear. Rather, the point which is stressed is that they are two "literal" and "visible" parts of the plan of God, and if they do in any way overlap it is "in a spiritual rather than a literal sense." This is merely historic premillennialism. All that was said by Nicholson and Imbrie could be consistently subscribed to by Lummis. It might also be added by way of confirming this conclusion that his numerous references and quotations in this essay are not from dispensationalist sources.

The hair-splitting definitions—the consequence of a mechanical view of inspiration—so common today are not much in evidence among these men. For example, there is no hard and fast distinction between "Kingdom of God," "Kingdom of Heaven," and "Kingdom of Christ." In general they make a more sound and scholarly hermeneutical approach than the later leaders of the movement. They refer readily to the original language of the New Testament, and they are much more cautious in establishing minute points of interpretation.

In summary it may be said that the Biblical view concerning the course of the ages is the paramount issue around which the thought of these men is oriented. The question which is of immediate importance and gives the issue relevance is, What is God's purpose for the Church in this age? The answer to this question in turn is important because it will determine the strategy and to some extent the message of the Church. If it is to expect a millennium as the result of its efforts and is to work toward that end, then more direct political and social action could be justified. If not, then the growing social concern and action on the part of some of the leaders like Henry Ward Beecher and Washington Gladden was a mistake and would lead ultimately to the defeat and ruin of Christianity.

Though Duffield, a professor of mathematics at Princeton College, said that the problem was "a purely Scriptural one,"[17] by which I assume he meant that the problem was basically one of hermeneutics and not of theology or philosophy, yet it is apparent that the whole complex of traditional Calvinistic theology is integrally involved. S. H. Kellogg went so far as to say that premillennialism was only applying the Augustinian view of the microcosm to the macrocosm.[18]

In conclusion, several general observations can be made about dispensationalism in the conference. One, it is not a central issue, nor is it considered an integral part of premillennialism. It is used as an argument to establish the main point at issue. Two, while the language of dispensationalism is evident in some instances, it is clear that the speakers who use it often do not understand or accept all of its implications as they have been elaborated in the years since then.

The Prophecy Conference of 1886

The conference of 1878 had been such a tremendous success that the men who had arranged for it decided to continue the existence of their committee in readiness to call another one at the opportune moment. From the report it appears that they anticipated calling another one quite soon, but it was eight years before these plans actually were realized. Prophecy continued to be a popular subject for discussion at the annual meetings of the Believers' Meetings for Bible Study, and in 1885 a conference especially for the discussion of prophetic subjects was planned to precede the annual Believers' Meeting at Niagara. This meeting was in charge of the leaders from Canada, and as far as one can tell it did not draw large crowds. The subjects covered the usual range, beginning with a paper on the history of the doctrine and ending with a series on the relation of the second coming of Christ to the resurrection, the Kingdom, Israel, and the mission of the Church.

One item of special interest to us appears in Brookes' report of the discussions at this conference. He says that one of the speakers took the position that only those who look for the rapture and long for its coming will take part in it. Brookes comments that the speaker "would not perhaps be sustained by most of the brethren who heard him,"[19] but he is very warm in his general commendation of the paper. Alas, the disapproval of Brookes and his associates was not sufficient to silence this most unfortunate doctrine.

In all of his reports and announcements published in *The Truth* in 1885, there is no mention whatsoever of a second international prophecy rally. In light of his usual policy of announcing such meetings far in advance in order to make special requests for prayer, it seems likely that late in 1885 there were still no plans for such a meeting. George C. Needham, who served as the secretary for the second conference, says only that it was called in response to many requests that had come to the men who planned the first one. The suspicion that the conference was rather hastily planned is heightened by a perusal of the program and a general reading of the papers submitted. At any rate, the committee which had planned the first conference was expanded to include thirteen other men, and a call went out for a second conference to be held in Chicago on November 16-20, 1886.

Needham, like West before him, not only acted as secretary of the conference but also accepted the responsibility for editing the essays and seeing that they were published. In his preface to the essays, published under the title *Prophetic Studies of the International Prophecy Conference,* Needham says that hundreds of men, including some postmillennialists, endorsed the call. He was convinced that since the conference in 1878 the doctrine of the "Lord's expected advent has gained ground among spiritual believers of all churches, as no other truth in modern times has done."

The conference convened Tuesday morning in Farwell Hall with "ministers of all denominations from all parts of the United States and Canada" present. Also "nearly all the city clergy were present, and hundreds of earnest Christians of every shade of belief from every church, charitable institution, and missionary society in the city."[20] It is thus quite clear from this report—even allowing for the probability that its general terms suggest maximums rather than minimums—and from an analysis of the denominational affiliation of the conference speakers, that this conference like the first one was interdenominational. It is interesting to note that at least half of the speakers at the conference were either Presbyterians or Baptists.

The reasons given for holding the conference are much the same as those given for the conference in 1878. The following is a summary of the reasons given by the secretary, Needham. (1) "To give prominence to neglected truth." (2) "To emphasize the true principles of Scripture interpretation." (3) To awaken Christians from slumber. (4) To present "the most majestic of all motives for world-wide evangelism." (5) To call attention to "the doctrine of 'last things' as a bulwark against the skepticism of modern theology." (6) To provide a real fellowship for "thousands of our Lord's dear saints who love his appearing and kingdom."[21]

The over-all plan of the conference was similar to that of the preceding one. On the whole the addresses seem to be of a more popular nature and the atmosphere more informal. The publication of the papers read at this conference was done very hastily, and the whole impression from a comparison of the two reports is that the first conference was of a much more scholarly nature. However, one cannot make a conclusive judgment about this from the two publications.

The Prophecy Conference seems to have been concluded on Saturday. At the close the resolutions of the 1878 conference were reaffirmed, and a resolution providing for a planning committee to arrange for a future conference was added. Regular church services were held Sunday morning, and on Sunday afternoon the conference reconvened as a missions conference, at which time W. E. Blackstone gave the main address.

The references to distinctly dispensational doctrines are more numerous in the proceedings of this conference than in the one held in 1878. Two distinct dispensational schemes are set forth, one by A. J. Frost and the other by W. E. Blackstone. Both of these men, one speaking on conditions in the world when Christ comes and the other on missions, use their doctrine to prove the progressive evil tendency of the present age. Much that was said about Parsons' discussion in 1878 would apply to Frost.

W. E. Blackstone's outline is practically identical to Scofield's with its seven "aions." Further, and more important, he has picked out what he considers to be the distinguishing feature of each dispensation. A statement made in his speech also suggests that he held the view later espoused by Scofield that there are different methods of salvation in each dispensation. He says, "Now whatever salvation God may have for the heathen by the law of conscience, as stated in Rom. 2:14-15, none of them can become members of this body or bride of Christ without hearing the gospel."[22] He also says, "We believe there is no key to Scripture more potent than this [recognition of dispensations]."[23]

A. T. Pierson, who had declared himself an adherent of the premillennial view in 1882 and is well known today as one of the consulting editors of the *Scofield Reference Bible,* appeared on the program. It is clear from his talk that he had already espoused the dispensationalist viewpoint by this time. He used dispensational arguments for two purposes. The first is the same as has been mentioned earlier. The second, which is latent in earlier arguments and assumptions, is to point out the "dispensational character" of Christ's first coming. He says, "Our Lord's coming is marked in Scripture teaching by its dispensational character. It marks a transition; it closes one dispensation and opens another. To understand this dispensational character is of primary importance."[24] He then proceeds in a characteristically dispensational manner to explain God's purpose in the present dispensation—to call out from among the Gentiles a people.

He maintains that there is a structural similarity in the different dispensations. For example, he says:

> The careful student of Scripture . . . finds dispensation succeeds dispensation in human history, all marked by seven features essentially the same. First, an advance in fullness and clearness of revelation; then gradual spiritual declension: then conformity to the world ending with amalgamation with the world; then a gigantic civilization, brilliant but Godless; then parallel development of evil and good; then an apostasy, and finally a catastrophe.[25]

But these "seven features essentially the same" in each dispensation are merely structural similarities, and as such are not essential to his concept of a dispensation. Fundamental differences between the dispensations begin to come into focus. Each dispensation features differences in the nature and method of God's dealings with men. There are differing purposes and differing rewards. This is all characteristic of contemporary dispensationalism.

There are evidences of distinctly dispensational beliefs in other speeches. H. M. Parsons of Toronto, Ontario, who was a familiar teacher in the Believers' Bible Meeting, is back with a well-developed dispensational view. J. S. Kennedy, a newcomer from the Southern Methodist Church in Abingdon, Virginia, seems to be a convinced dispensationalist. Many of the speakers assume that the Kingdom is not present and is something entirely different from the Church. Depending upon the general context of such teaching, a distinction between the two might be interpreted as merely historic premillennialism, but one gains the impression that more is inherent here. J. G. Princell teaches the Darbyite doctrine of the pretribulation rapture, which is closely associated with Scofield dispensationalism. It is clear that some others also believe this doctrine, though the nature of their papers does not lead them to state it explicitly. Still others are quite explicit in their description of the millennium as a Jewish heyday. For example, G. S. Bishop says:

> Focalize the Scriptures, and they teach that all the lines of God's eternal purposes as to the future blessing of the world meet their fulfillment—not mystically in Christianity and figuratively through the church, but literally after the church has been caught away into heaven—in the restoration of the Jews, God's chosen earthly people to their original and promised land.[26]

Reference to the Kingdom coming after the Church "has been caught away into heaven" and to the Jews as God's *"earthly* people" gives this statement a distinctly dispensationalist flavor.

Bishop W. R. Nicholson, whom we met at the conference of 1878, clearly teaches that Jesus withdrew His offer of the Kingdom to the Jewish people in the latter part of His ministry. He says:

> Where, then, is this kingdom? It is not yet. It will be inaugurated at Christ's second coming. For while, in His earlier ministry, the Lord Jesus offered to the Jewish people the kingdom of heaven as nigh at hand, yet, at a later date, and because of their rejecting Him, His preaching of the kingdom underwent a remarkable change. It was no longer nigh at hand; it had been postponed . . .
>
> "The kingdom of heaven is like a sower" . . . and is understood by many to mean that the kingdom of heaven is present in this dispensation. On the contrary . . .
>
> No, the kingdom of God is not now.[27]

This language suggests that Nicholson had made considerable progress toward a more integrated dispensationalist position since the first conference. As was pointed out in connection with his discussion at the 1878 conference, his basic position seems to have been that of historic premillennialism. In a footnote to that paper he does refer to "the whole period between the First and Second Advents being a parenthesis between the sixty-ninth and seventieth of these [Daniel's] prophetic weeks."[28] But this type of postponement is not necessarily dispensational, and the other comments in this discussion give definite evidence that he had not been greatly influenced by dispensationalist teaching at that time. The statements quoted above indicate definite influence. This is precisely what William Kelly and other Plymouth Brethren were teaching. How far the process of assimilation had proceeded is difficult to say. He still fails to make the distinction between "Kingdom of God," "Kingdom of Christ," "Kingdom of Heaven," and "Kingdom of David," which is characteristic of contemporary dispensationalists.

However, it is evident that not all the men at the conference are of this persuasion. Men like Nathaniel West, John T. Duffield, and A. J. Gordon ally themselves with the historic premillennial position of European commentators like Meyer, Godet, and Delitzsch. Nathaniel West read letters from some of these men to the people at the conference. He had received the letters in answer to questions which he had sent out. Delitzsch said that he was in general agreement with his American premillennial brethren, but that he believed "in the literal reality of this apocalyptic picture *without pressing slavishly the letter.*"[29] In his letter Delitzsch also repudiated the idea of a Jewish national restoration. After reading this to the conference, West added his supporting comment saying that he was sure that "all" present cordially sympathized with the protest of Dr. Delitzsch against a reproduction of the Jewish Old Testament earthly and national theocracy.[30] In saying "all," West was no doubt overly optimistic. However, on the same subject James Orrock, an Adventist editor of the *Messiah's Herald,* quotes George N. H. Peters as also against this view, and says that he himself was led to take the same position as Peters "many years ago." In answer to those who object to premillennialism because of this particular tenet, he says further, "There are many premillennialists, however, who do not hold to the restoration of these bloody sacrifices during the millennium."

On the subject of the Kingdom and the Church, West argues for the Kingdom as a present reality, though only a partial fulfillment of what will be completely fulfilled later. This is in direct contrast to Nicholson's remarks.

Over against the dark picture of the Church as fast slipping into apostasy, A. J. Gordon says that the Church's light only shines the brighter in the surrounding darkness. He likens the Church to the newly invented electric light "so surpassingly brilliant," and continues, "Now, I make bold to say that the Church of Jesus Christ . . . never since the apostolic age has shed a purer and more widely diffused light upon the world than she is doing today."[31] Bishop Maurice Baldwin of Canada says of the Anglican Church that "never was there a time of deeper spiritual life—never was there a time of intenser earnestness than there is today . . ."[32] The revived interest in missions is to him a sign of Jesus' near return.

Latent in this difference is another, viz., whether the "rapture" of the saints will be before the tribulation period or after it. Darby held that the organized Church would become apostate and would have to enter the tribulation, while the saints who had come out from the apostasy would be caught up with Christ before the time of tribulation. The saints who would be caught up with Christ were those who were looking for Him, and this might occur at any moment since much of the prophecy concerning Christ's second coming would be fulfilled after the rapture.

One of the specific issues involved in this difference of opinion is the coming and character of the Antichrist. The questions are whether or not he has already come, whether he will come before Christ returns to take away the Church, and whether he will be an outgrowth of the Jewish or the Christian religion. Darby held that he will come after the rapture as the product of a completely apostate Church. As was noted before, there is evidence that this viewpoint was held by some of the speakers at the conference. On the other hand, men like Gordon and Duffield, who were of the historic school, explicitly disagreed with it. Gordon held that "the Man of Sin" is to be identified with the papacy. He called on his brethren to search the Scriptures anew and to be sure before they gave up their testimony "against the Man of Rome as Antichrist."[33]

Against the argument that one could not believe in the imminence of Christ's coming and at the same time hold to the theory of a post-tribulation rapture, Duffield countered that the Apostle Paul had done so. He quoted Meyer who says, "It is incontestable, as the result of correct exegesis, that Paul not only considered Antichrist as directly preceding the advent, but also regarded the advent as so near, that he himself might be alive." He followed this quotation with a paragraph showing that it is "conclusive" that Paul did not consider the imminence of Christ's coming to be inconsistent with the prediction of certain events yet to take place.[34]

This cleavage between the two groups became still more clearly defined in the years which followed, but as long as A. J. Gordon and J. H. Brookes were alive it did not come to an open break. Gordon held a somewhat mediating position so that after his death both sides claimed him. Brookes went much further with his dispensational interpretation, but he held firmly to his denominational concept of the Church.

The pessimism already evident in the conference of 1878 has grown to alarmist proportions. W. E. Blackstone, A. T. Pierson, and others paint the darkest possible pictures of civilization, and even of the Church. One example is enough to illustrate the temper of the more openly dispensational brethren:

> Two-thirds of nominal Christendom is one vast overshadowing hierarchy, a system of Mariolatry, if not of idolatry, with a false ritualism, and a grossly materialistic sacramentarianism, while the remaining third of the professed church is sadly compromised by rationalism in its theology, and humanitarianism

in its Christology. Outside the church and within, spiritualism enrolls its millions; annihilationism and second probationism, a kind of "incipient, theological dry rot," boast their thousands, hundreds of whom stand in so-called orthodox pulpits, and openly proclaim these false doctrines, or secretly entertain them.

. . . A thousand pulpits are drifting from the doctrine of inspiration, the deity of Christ, the vicarious atonement, the resurrection of the body, and eternal retribution. Nearly the whole church, Catholic and Protestant, in the United States has drifted away from the apostolic doctrine of Christ's premillennial advent. . . . Wanted, a man in all our religious schools to teach the entire system of prophetic and dispensational truth![35]

By and large, what one might call the dispensationalist mood had settled over the assembly. This is no doubt due to two things. On the one hand, the writings of the Plymouth Brethren, which are a first-class exhibit of utter pessimism, had gained a wider reading and had made a more profound impression. On the other hand, it was during this period of eight years that theological liberalism and what was later to be called the "Social Gospel" made great strides ahead in the seminaries and pulpits of America. For example, the controversy at Andover Seminary was in full swing. Many of these issues were being given space in the press, so that the debate had descended to the intellectual level of the laity in general. All of this had made the conservative pastors and evangelists of which this movement consisted keenly aware of the growing opposition which they faced.

In the beginning the movement was an endeavor to recapture a forgotten truth, and pessimism was more or less a matter of principle. The dispensational argument was an extremely handy tool to use in destroying the shallow optimism of an overweening postmillennialism, while the postmillennial opponents were usually considered brothers in the faith. But these characteristics were less and less in evidence. In 1886 there was a new note of urgency. The eschatological hope was now set as a "bulwark against the skepticism of modern theology." Needham wrote:

The gentlemen at Andover feel deeply aggrieved that their smoky and sulphurous match-light of mongrel Ayrian-German

[sic] rationalism is not readily utilized by those who walk in the undimmed sunlight of divine revelation as it shines in every verse, word, and letter from Gen. 1 to Rev. 22. Brethren, premillenarianism pure and simple forms a breakwater against every advancing tide which would throw upon the clean beach of a God-given theology the jelly-fish theories evolved out of man's erratic consciousness, pride, and self-will.[36]

It was during this period of growing antagonism and controversy that most of the men who played a decisive part in the development of contemporary dispensationalism joined the movement. They read the writings of the Plymouth Brethren in a historical context that seemed fully to justify their pessimism, and they accepted their dispensational tenets almost as the essence of orthodoxy. To men of their temperament a mediating position seemed dangerous, to say the least. But this takes us ahead of our story. We now need to return to the later developments in the Believers' Meeting for Bible Study.

6. THE DECLINE OF THE NIAGARA BIBLE CONFERENCE

Under the leadership of Brookes the Believers' Meeting for Bible Study continued to meet annually. For three years (1878-1880) it was held at Clifton Springs, New York. In 1881 the group moved to Old Orchard, Maine, and in 1882 to Mackinac Island on the northern edge of Michigan. Gaebelein says that this move was for the benefit of the Canadian brethren.[1] Then for the next fifteen years (1883-1897), the conference was held at Niagara-on-the-Lake, Ontario, from which it received the name Niagara Conference. This town provided excellent facilities and was easily accessible by train or lake steamer since it was only a few miles from the Niagara Falls. In 1898 the group met at Point Chautauqua. The last regular meeting was held in 1900 at Asbury Park, New Jersey.

The immediate cause for the decline of the Niagara Conference was the death of A. J. Gordon in 1895 and of J. H. Brookes in 1897. Brookes had been the president of the conference for years, and had held the movement together even though there was a growing divergence of opinion. Before we tell the story of the closing of the conference in 1901, we should trace the development of this cleavage within the group, which was one of the main causes for its dissolution.

As was noted before, the innovations in the premillennial outline of end-time events—namely, the pretribulation secret rapture of the Church and its corollary, the "any-moment theory" which Darby taught—were introduced into Canada and the United States in the 1860's and 1870's, and apparently became an accepted part of the premillennial teaching of the Believers' Meeting. It is not clear whether all the early leaders endorsed the theory wholeheartedly or not, but at least until about 1883 or 1884 there was little or no verbal dissent. About this time Nathaniel West was privately challenged by Robert Cameron concerning the Scriptural validity of the "any-moment theory," which states that Christ might have returned to earth at *any moment* since His ascension. West had uncritically accepted this theory, although he had not held to the pretribulation rapture of the Church. Cameron, a Baptist minister and member of the planning committee for the Bible conference, had himself been in doubt about the teaching for some time, but it was not until he came into contact with the writings of B. W. Newton, S. P. Tregelles, and George Müller—leaders of the Plymouth Brethren who had rejected Darby's ideas on this point—that his views on the subject were crystallized enough to challenge the conference's position. Cameron related the incident years later in his book, *Scriptural Truth About the Lord's Return.*

> About the year 1883, the writer was pastor of Park Baptist Church, Brantford, Canada, and having attended the Clifton Springs, afterwards Niagara Conference, was appointed one of the committee of nine to take charge of subjects, speakers and other matters. At the 1884 Conference it came to be the "fashion" of every speaker to "ring the changes" on the possibility of Christ Coming any moment—before the morning dawned, before the meeting closed, and even before the speaker had completed his address. Feeling that this was utterly unscriptural and dangerous, the writer opened his heart to the late Dr. Nathaniel West, the greatest and most exhaustive student of the Bible and of historic theology, among the teachers participating in the Conference. When pressed for the reason, it was frankly made known, and this led the Doctor to accompany the writer to his room in the "Annex." We talked and prayed until beyond two o'clock in the morning. After walking the floor backwards and forwards in silence, the great man stopped, pointed his finger at me and said: "Cameron, I begin to think you are right. I will give these matters careful and exhaustive attention, and if I find that the Scriptures teach contrary to what is taught in this Conference, I will reverse myself and boldly defend the truth."[2]

Apparently West did what he promised. It was not long after this that he began a vigorous attack on the "any-moment theory." In 1892 he published a twelve-page pamphlet entitled *The Coming of the Lord in the "Teaching of the Twelve Apostles,"* and in 1893 a thirty-four-page pamphlet, *The Apostle Paul and the "Any-Moment Theory."* In both of these he repudiated the teaching, attacking it on both historical and Biblical grounds.

Gaebelein, who was an ardent dispensationalistic premillennialist at the time, relates an incident involving himself and West in another night discussion about 1897 or 1898. He says:

> . . . I roomed with Dr. West, but it was a sleepless night; only towards five in the morning did I get some rest. Dr. West was a great scholar and strong advocate of the premillennial coming of our Lord. But we differed on the church and the great tribulation.
>
> Unlike Brookes, Gordon, Parsons, Needham, myself and others, Dr. West believed that the church would be on earth till the very end of that period of trouble. He tried hard to win me over to his side. . . . It was a hot conflict which strengthened greatly my belief in my view, which I believe is based on Scripture. We were good friends.[3]

Both Cameron, who succeeded A. J. Gordon as editor of *The Watchword,* and West continued to attack the theory in their publications and at the Niagara Conference. In 1897 Cameron noted that "lately a great reaction was come."[4] Among the men who he says had the courage to reverse themselves were Nathaniel West, W. G. Moorehead, W. J. Erdman, J. M. Stifler, [Henry W.?] Frost, and A. J. Gordon.[5] Cameron personally sought to persuade both Gordon and Brookes, and though he did not claim to have completely won Brookes, he did feel that he was moving toward a "harmonistic" position in the last few years of his life.

This difference of opinion was more than a surface rift over certain technical distinctions. West said that within the premillennial fold there was being fostered "a brood of heresies, scarcely less numerous than the sum total of all that appeared in the first four centuries of the Christian Church."[6] He objected to the evangelical men who were crying the ruin of the Church, and accused them of actually joining hands with the higher critics and sceptics who were also sure of the downfall of the Church.[7] In a similar attack in the February, 1897, issue of *The Watchword* he said that they were playing into the hands of the agnostics because their theories actually made Jesus contradict Himself. As the issues cleared, Cameron directly attacked the practice of cataloguing New Testament passages into dispensational divisions.

Though the debate often raged over the more incidental aspects of the argument, the indications are that these men made a fundamental break with dispensationalism. They differed with the sharp dispensational distinction between the Kingdom and the Church, which is the basic issue, and with their mechanical, dispensational method of interpreting the Bible. It is quite interesting that West and Cameron noticed what has since become more clearly evident to scholars; namely, that the dispensational interpretation rests on the same type of linguistic assumptions and analytical methods as the earlier higher critical interpretation, and that both schools of thought arrived at similar conclusions even though they began from antithetical theological positions. The dispensationalists were men of their time working at the problems of their time, and from a modern vantage point it appears that their mistake was not that they sought to preserve the fundamental insights of traditional Christianity, but that they used inferior tools. George Ricker Berry compares them to paleolithic men with their stone axes trying to build a modern skyscraper.[8]

To return to the story of the Niagara Conference, Brookes died in April, 1897, after the plans had been made for the twenty-first annual conference to be held the next summer. Notice of the meeting was published in the last (May) issue of *The Truth*. The nature of the meeting and personnel are described in the notice.

> The Conference, as usual, will devote the entire time to the study of the Sacred Scriptures. The studies will be in the Minor Prophets and in the Epistle [sic] of Paul to the Churches.

The following named brethren have been chosen to con-
duct the studies this year: W. J. Erdman, E. P. Goodwin, F. E.
Howitt, W. G. Moorehead, G. C. Needham, H. M. Parsons,
C. I. Scofield, E. F. Stroeter.[9]

The meeting was held as scheduled, and a full report was
published in the first issue of *The Watchword and Truth* (July
and August, 1897).[10] The notice of the conference for 1898 announced that besides the regular Bible studies "other hours will
be devoted to the Dispensations in relation to the coming of
Christ, the Hope of the Church and the Hope of Israel . . ."[11]
The content of these discussions was not reported by Cameron.
No report of the 1899 conference appeared in *The Watchword
and Truth,* but some of the discussions were published as
articles.[12]

The attendance at the meetings began to fall off from 1898
on. In 1900 Cameron noted that there was a "marked absence
of young people," and further that "the number of evangelists
and pastors did not seem so great as in former years." More serious yet, he felt that there was an "evident absence of fervor and
depth of conviction which marked the teaching of former years."
He urged that a group of the preachers and teachers meet privately for discussion and prayer.[13] Such a meeting was held in
Brooklyn in the fall of 1900, with W. J. Erdman presiding. After
a discussion of the variations in prophetic interpretations which
existed among them, some agreement seems to have been reached.
It was decided to hold two smaller Bible study conferences the
coming year instead of a single large one. The first conference
was planned for the coming winter, and was to be held in some
large centrally located city. The second one was to be held at
a resort during the following summer.[14] The winter meeting
apparently was held as scheduled, but the following May (1901),
instead of issuing a call for the summer conference, the committee announced its decision not to send out a call. Their only explanation was that many smaller local and more specialized Bible
study conferences had come into existence and had drawn interest

away from the larger central meeting. With this explanation the Niagara Conference expired.

The justification given by the committee for discontinuing the conference was pretty clearly only part of the total reason. Though it was not explicitly stated, one can read between the lines that there was increasing tension among the leaders of the movement in the closing years. Scofield himself admitted that this disagreement was one of the causes contributing to the closing of the conference.[15]

Though a large number of the men in the movement continued to work together under the banner of premillennialism, two more or less distinct groups formed, with C. I. Scofield and A. C. Gaebelein as the champions of dispensationalism. With Scofield's help, Gaebelein secured the mailing lists of *The Truth* and advertised his magazine, *Our Hope,* as the doctrinal successor to it. He justified himself in this by claiming that Cameron was not faithfully carrying on in the prophetic witness of Brookes and Gordon. Further, Scofield and Gaebelein formed a nucleus for a new conference organization. In 1901, with the financial support of some wealthy Plymouth Brethren, they began the Sea Cliff Bible Conference which continued for ten years. It was this group that planned the prophecy conferences at Chicago in 1914 and at New York in 1918. The dispensationalists had won the day so completely that for the next fifty years friend and foe alike largely identified dispensationalism with premillennialism.

Kingdom or Church

While there are many minor points of difference between historic and dispensational premillennialism, the crucial difference is the doctrine of the Church. This was not immediately apparent to the pioneers of the prophetic conference movement. At first dispensationalism seemed to be a useful weapon in the debate with postmillennialism. In America it developed within the premillennial fold as an argument against postmillennialism's identification of the Kingdom and the Church. A distinction between the two was made in historic premillennialism, but they were not so completely divorced as in dispensationalism. In no other area is the difference between the nature and emphasis of historic premillennialism and dispensationalism more clearly seen. Postmillennialism equated the Kingdom and the Church. Historic premillennialism refused to equate them, but held that by definition they overlapped and were historically related. Dispensationalism completely separated them and made the Kingdom uppermost. James E. Bear succinctly points out the difference between the latter two.

> Both believed in a Kingdom of Christ on earth after His Return. But the historic Premillennialist exalted the Church and held that the Church enjoyed the Kingdom. If the Jews were to have any place of preeminence, it was because of their Christian zeal. If they were to enjoy the Kingdom, it was because they had become a part of the Church.
>
> Modern Premillennialists, following the Dispensational lead, make the Kingdom a Jewish Kingdom, given to the Jews because they are Jews. The Church has become a special group, different in character and destiny from those who enjoy the Kingdom.[16]

On the practical level this distinction called for a redefinition of the nature and purpose of the Church. The postmillennialists believed that the Church represented God's ultimate plan for society, that the world was to be improved and that the final phase of the Kingdom, the millennium, was to be ushered in by the work of the Holy Spirit through the Church. Historic premillennialism held essentially the same concept of the Church, but made a less optimistic prognosis. The Kingdom would not be brought in by the work of the Church, but by the arrival of the King. Dispensationalism offered a reactionary solution which, to use William Marshall Horton's description of Barth's reaction to liberalism, managed to be wrong at every point where the postmillennialists were wrong, but in the opposite sense.[17]

This redefinition seems to have proceeded as follows: In the first place, the dispensational arguments were used to justify the premillennial predictions about this dispensation. They argued that since all the dispensations preceding this one had followed the same pattern and ended in failure, there was no reason to believe that this one would be different. The dispensations were not precisely defined or numbered. This was relatively unimportant. The main thing was to outline a dispensational or age pattern which could be projected upon the present age as a means of forecasting the course of this age.

Many of the men who used dispensationalism for this purpose were still thinking and working within the framework of the older concepts of the Church and its relation to the world. They used a vocabulary without following logically all of its implications as they were later developed. They were often not aware of the implicit inconsistencies between their new arguments and the traditional concepts. They tended to use dispensational arguments at some specific points, but did not make them an integral part of their system.

In the more advanced stage of development, the dispensational divisions were used to redefine the nature and purpose of the Church. The Church was thought of as that elect group of individuals who were selected or gathered out of the world during this age to receive spiritual blessings and a heavenly reward as the bride of Christ. These elect individuals were not to be equated with the personnel of any visible Church organization. In contrast to the Kingdom, the Church was defined as a spiritual unity. Accordingly, interdenominational unity did not mean co-operation between denominations. It meant, rather, that individual Christians should not restrict their fellowship and co-operation to denominational organizations. This emphasis upon the gathered-out individual minimized the importance of the corporate aspects of the Church's life and subtly undermined loyalty to the existing denominations.

The task of the Church was defined also within the limits of its purely spiritual existence. The Church's task, it was taught, is not self-propagation since the saved community is not an end in itself to be achieved in this world. Missions are not for the purpose of extending the borders of the Church, but for the "out-gathering" of other elect individuals. In their own words, the work of the Church was described as "evangelism" rather than "conversion" of the world. By evangelism they meant verbal witness to the message of the Scriptures. A. T. Pierson quoted the Scripture, "Go ye into all the world, and preach the gospel to every creature," and then commented, "There our commission begins and ends. With results we have nothing to do, and are incapable of tracing or guaging them."[18] W. E. Blackstone said, "This testimony, then, is the Word of God and the testimony of the believer, or, in other words, the open Bible and the preacher or proclaimer."[19] He challenged the people to this work by saying, "Think of it! All the millions of the unevangelized might hear the gospel in twelve months if there were only preachers to declare it."[20] A. J. Frost said, "Both post and premillennialists have committed the great error of spending ages to educate and Christianize a part of the world instead of evangelizing the whole world."[21] Pierson pretty well summed it up when he said:

> . . . But the church is not to stop to convert any part of the world, but to go through the world to evangelize it, preaching to every creature so that all men may hear . . . its province is to be a witness to the world; the whole field is to be sown with the seed of the kingdom, and we are not to wait to secure full harvests at one corner of the world and let the rest of the world lie unsown.[22]

If the building of the Church community could not be justified as a part of the Church's task, there was even less justification for social action. The Church should not spend her energy trying to solve the problems of a society that was doomed for destruction. The Church is a separated group, despised and persecuted by the world. "The gospel of the kingdom is to be preached, not to improve the present condition of the world, but to save men out from it; not to court its approval and admiration, but to incur the hatred of the world by showing up its death nature and its inborn devilish tendencies."[23]

The argument was carried a step further by some who depreciated the ability of the Church to carry out such a task as the conversion of the world. In a characteristic passage E. F. Stroeter said:

> No, not the mortal, fallible, erring church, whose knowing is in part and whose prophesying is in part. . . . Not the mortal, divided, scattered, broken church, which partly from want of love, partly through unavoidable imperfection, partly through death and the grave has never been able, and never will be able this side of her resurrection to demonstrate to the world the wonderful reality of her oneness in and with Christ her head—shall bring an adoring world to the Redeemer's feet.[24]

Others estimated the total working force of Christians at about one-tenth of total Christendom, or one-fifth of Protestantism. It was pointed out that in spite of the valiant effort of missionaries throughout the history of the Church, the number of unconverted men and women increased in proportion to the world's population. They felt that this fact in itself should stir Christians to rethink the purpose, method, and motivation for their task.

The only incentive that could be offered in a situation like this was the command itself. Christ had given the task, and the results were not the province of the servants. Some suggestion was made that the coming of the Lord might be hastened by the faithful execution of preaching the gospel, but this was not the first or main motivation offered.

The results of this redefinition were far-reaching, and indicate the real nature of the movement. In emphasizing the heavenly and future aspect of Christians' rewards they destroyed the balance between two equally important aspects of the Church's life; namely, the Church as a saved community being an *end* in the world, and the Church as a witnessing community being a *means* to an end. For them the Kingdom rather than the Church represented the end of God's program in the world. The Church exists as a sort of guerrilla resistance movement awaiting the army of liberation. As a consequence its strategy—to continue the figure—is worked out along the lines of guerrilla tactics. Thus the social implications of the gospel were ignored, and evangelism was defined in terms which excluded the building of the church community. Emphasis was placed on getting "decisions for Christ," which meant accepting the essential concept that Christ forgives the sinner his personal offenses. A pietistic, individualistic type of Christian experience was cultivated, with relatively less stress being given to the ethical relevance of the experience. And lastly, denominational loyalties were broken down. Members of the "true Church" found their fellowship at interdenominational levels in the Bible conferences and the like. Leaders of the movement more and more worked on an interdenominational or nondenominational basis. "Faith" missions, Bible institutes, and other individualistic projects which sprang up claimed the support of congregations and individual members, and a rash of cheap magazines and papers published by leading evangelists or Bible teachers in the movement supplied the reading material upon which they fed. Like the proverbial cuckoo's egg, dispensationalism was hatched in the nest of premillennialism, and when hatched it soon completely dominated the nest.

Conclusion

In 1888 S. H. Kellogg wrote an article defending premillennialism in which he pointed out that many of the doctrines which were associated with the premillennialist position by its critics were merely vagaries of the system. He summed up the fundamental theological position of historic premillennialism in four succinct points, and even a cursory reading of these shows clearly that dispensational distinctions are not a vital part of the doctrine. These four points are as follows:

(1) The Scriptures teach us to expect on the earth a universal triumph of the gospel, and a prolonged supremacy of righteousness and truth.

(2) They also teach that we are to expect a personal, visible return of the risen and ascended Christ, in the glory of his Father.

(3) The teachings of the Scripture forbid us to place the predicted reign of righteousness on this side of the personal

advent; they therefore compel us to place it on the other side of that event. Whence it follows that we must conclude that—

(4) The purpose of the return of Christ to the earth is to set up and administer the promised kingdom of righteousness, by establishing over the whole earth a theocratic government, vested in the Son of man and his risen and glorified people who shall have believed on him up to the time of his appearing.[25]

Kellogg considered such doctrines as "the restoration of Israel, and the position of that nation in the expected new order of things; the interpretation of the prophecies concerning the antichrist; the distinction in time between the resurrection of the righteous and that of the wicked, etc.,"[26] to be doctrines more or less associated with this position. All of these, of course, are very closely associated with dispensationalism. It is into this category of peripheral doctrines that all the rest of the dispensational distinctions must also be classified. Premillennialism can be defined as a theological entity distinct from its dispensational trappings; and historically, it has been so defined and defended apart from dispensationalism. This interpretation of the relation between the two positions has been verified by recent developments within the premillennialist camp. I refer to the growing awareness among them that the dispensationalist interpretation of the Kingdom and Church is not entirely satisfactory. In spite of the long-standing claim made by some contemporary dispensationalists that all premillennialists must of logical necessity be dispensationalists, the opinion to the contrary seems to be gaining ground.

7. SCOFIELD'S SYNTHESIS

Probably no other one man has been more influential in spreading dispensational teachings than C. I. Scofield. Through his Bible study course, participation in Bible conferences, numerous magazine articles and pamphlets, and most of all through the *Scofield Reference Bible,* he popularized the doctrine throughout the United States and Canada. He did not claim originality for his work, and in this disclaimer he was correct. He clarified and standardized the work of others. Who, then, was this man, and where did he get his ideas?

Biographical Note and History of the Reference Bible

Cyrus Ingerson Scofield was born August 19, 1843, into the home of Daniel Scofield.[1] His mother died a short time after his birth, but he was reared by a Christian father who belonged to the Protestant Episcopal Church. During the Civil War he served with distinction as a Confederate soldier. After the war he studied law in St. Louis, Missouri, and was admitted to the Kansas bar in 1869. He entered Kansas politics for a while, and was appointed United States Attorney for Kansas by President Grant. After two years in this office he resigned and returned to St. Louis to practice law. It was here in 1879 that he was converted through the efforts of a Y.M.C.A. worker. Not long after his conversion he made the acquaintance of J. H. Brookes, who was a pastor in that city. Brookes helped him in his study of the Bible and introduced him to dispensational premillennialism.[2] It was here, Gaebelein says, that "he learned what he could not have learned in any of the theological seminaries of that time."[3] He had no formal Bible training before he began his work as a pastor, lecturer, and teacher.

In 1882 he was called to a small Congregational Church in Dallas, Texas, where he served till 1895 when he was called to East Northfield, Massachusetts. About this time he became active in the Niagara Bible Conference as a teacher. He was a popular speaker and was in great demand at the Bible conferences over the country. In 1903 he returned to his former pastorate in Dallas, where he began his work on the *Reference Bible*.

The idea of a reference Bible had been growing in his mind for some years prior to this, but lack of time and finances had forced him to delay the project. He had more than he could do during the years that he was writing the Bible course, and was often tardy with the completion of the different installments of the course. Then in 1902, at the request of A. C. Gaebelein, the men who were backing the Sea Cliff Conference decided to make finances available for the projected *Reference Bible*. With this assurance Scofield accepted the pastorate in Dallas, where he was relieved of some of his pastoral duties so that he could concentrate on the work of preparing the *Reference Bible*. The Bible was completed and ready for the public by 1909.

Scofield was convinced that the Bible could be easily understood by anyone if it were only studied according to its dispensational divisions. In 1902 he wrote, "The clear perception of this doctrine of the Ages makes a most important step in the progress of the student of the divine oracles. It has the same relation to the right understanding of the Scriptures that correct outline work has to map making."[4] In a sheet containing the purpose and plan for the projected *Reference Bible,* which he distributed to the consulting editors and others who were interested, he said that it was his plan "to prepare an edition of God's Holy Word so clearly and simply divided and arranged that any believer of ordinary intelligence may read the Bible understandingly," and "that ministers, evangelists, and advanced students may be led into a deeper knowledge of the Book."[5]

In line with this conviction and purpose, he arranged the text of his *Reference Bible* to indicate the dispensational and structural divisions as he conceived them. In addition, he supplied theological definitions of important Biblical words, brief notes on important Biblical themes and types, with special attention given to fulfilled and unfulfilled prophecy.

Of the seven consulting editors[6] Gaebelein was perhaps the most influential.[7] He and Scofield held almost identical views on most of the subjects, and Gaebelein was given a free hand in the interpretation of certain prophetic portions. According to the plan of procedure all the associate editors were to be consulted concerning the definitions included in the footnotes, and they were consulted on various other points; but Scofield reserved the right to draft the final wording and outlines. In the preface he exempts them from responsibility for what he has included, and we cannot assume, as Ehlert does, that all of them agreed fully with him.[8] In fact, it is clear that they did not.

One word more should be said about the direct influence of the Plymouth Brethren on Scofield and Gaebelein. Francis Fitch, and presumably Alwyn Ball and John T. Pirie, the men who made the project possible, were Plymouth Brethren. Fitch had a printing establishment, and he acted as publisher of the Scofield Bible Course during its first years. He also printed Gaebelein's magazine, *Our Hope*. Further, both Scofield and Gaebelein were thoroughly acquainted with the writings of the earlier Brethren. Gaebelein says that it was through the instrumentality of the men named above that he learned of the writings of Darby and others. He says, "I found in his [Darby's] writings, in the works of William Kelly, McIntosh [sic], F. W. Grant, Bellett and others the soul food I needed. *I esteem these men next to the Apostles* in their sound and spiritual teaching."[9] Scofield might have given the same type of testimony. Reese says of him that he was "for a generation an assiduous and admiring student of Darby's writings."[10]

Scofield's Dispensationalism

Scofield's dispensational definitions and outline have become the standard for contemporary American dispensationalism. The sharp criticism which a distinguished fundamentalist revision committee has received from some quarters for attempting even a slight revision of the notes in the *Reference Bible* indicates just how standard Scofield has become in the minds of thousands. Because of this it is necessary to examine his outline and general position in some detail, although he admittedly adds little that is distinctly new. His unique contribution is his organization of the data into a popular system.

Scofield makes a distinction not only between *age* and *dispensation* but also between *covenant* and *dispensation*. His explanatory notes on the subject are brief to the point of ambiguity, and his implicit assumptions and distinctions often have to be pieced together from numerous references and then filled out from the writings of men like Lewis Sperry Chafer, who have continued and amplified the system. Scofield defines a dispensation as "a period of time during which man is tested in respect of obedience to some *specific* revelation of the will of God."[11] Chafer merely justifies and enlarges on this definition by citing the definition given in the *Century Dictionary*.[12] Ehlert gives us additional insight when he seeks to clarify the difference between an age and a dispensation. Commenting on George Wilson's outline of the ages, he says:

> His scheme is properly to be included in a discussion of the dispensations, even though he calls his divisions "ages" *because they are conceived of as developing God's program of redemption.* We draw the dividing line between the twin doctrines of ages and dispensations at this point: *if time is divided into periods without respect to God's redemptive program, those divisions would be ages but not dispensations.*[13]

From this it is clear that a dispensation is not simply a chronological period of time. William Kelly stated it concisely when he said that a dispensation "means a certain course of time, *ruled by particular principles.*"[14] In fact, what is pointed out in all these statements is that the distinctive thing about a *dispensation* in contrast to an *age* is the nontemporal aspect. It is the fact that "particular principles" are in force or that a test "in respect of obedience to some specific revelation" is taking place which constitutes an age a dispensation. Thus it becomes apparent that what is involved here is a methodology of redemption, a rationale of God's dealings with mankind. The rationale is based on the "dispensational divisions" of humanity into the Jews, the Gentiles, and the Church. Some dispensations affect only the Jews; some Jews and Gentiles. Furthermore, these dispensations overlap in time. The Gentiles may be living under one dispensation —as in fact they are—while historically contemporary Christians and Jews are living under others. The coherence of Scofield's dispensational system is not historical or organic, but theological and schematic. It becomes historical only by virtue of being superimposed on the historical narrative.

Scofield outlines and describes the seven dispensations as follows:

1. *Innocency.* This dispensation is characterized by the Edenic covenant, which consists of God's instruction to Adam to procreate, subdue the earth, have dominion over all the animals, and eat of all the plants of the garden except the tree of the knowledge of good and evil. This last exception constituted the specific test during this dispensation. Man's failure to meet the test resulted in his judgment—the expulsion from the garden.

2. *Conscience.* Scofield explains that when man was created, he was ignorant of good and evil. His sin brought an awakening of conscience. After man was expelled from the garden he was placed under the Adamic covenant, which included the curse of Satan (the serpent) and the earth, physical death for man, and the promise of the Redeemer. In this dispensation man's test was to avoid all known evil according to his *conscience.* The dispensation ended in the judgment of the flood.

3. *Human Government.* During this dispensation man is submitted to the test of governing his fellow men for God. He is

given the right of capital punishment. Scofield says, "The highest function of government is the judicial taking of life." [15] This dispensation is characterized by the Noahic covenant.

The dispensation of human government continues in force and overlaps chronologically with other dispensations. The responsibility of human government rests on the whole race, and thus applies to the Jews in addition to the other responsibilities of later dispensations. For the Jews as a distinct nation, however, this dispensation ended with the captivities. For the Gentiles it will end at the judgment of the nations which is to take place just before the millennium begins.

4. *Promise.* This dispensation was inaugurated with the call of Abraham and the Abrahamic covenant. "That covenant is wholly gracious and unconditional." [16] It "founds the nation of Israel, and confirms, with specific additions, the Adamic promise of redemption." [17] "The Dispensation of Promise extends from Gen. 12:1 to Ex. 19:8, and was exclusively Israelitish." [18] Scofield does not explicitly state what the dispensational test is for this period of time. Presumably the test is faith in God's promise after the analogy of the dispensation of grace, which is its extension and fulfillment. Evidently the affliction in Egypt is the judgment, but we are told that this dispensation did not end until Israel "rashly" accepted the law and said, "All that the Lord hath said will we do, and be obedient." [19]

5. *Law.* The covenant which conditions the life of Israel during this period is the Mosaic. It is characterized as "moral" and "conditional." However, Scofield says, "The Law did not abrogate the Abrahamic Covenant, but was an intermediate disciplinary dealing 'till the Seed should come to whom the promise was made.' " [20] This dispensation applies exclusively to Israel, and extends to the cross. The Gentiles during this period remain in the dispensation of human government. The test for this dispensation is "legal obedience as the condition of salvation." [21] As in the other cases, man fails and is judged.

6. *Grace.* "As a dispensation, grace begins with the death and resurrection of Christ. The point of testing is no longer legal obe-

dience as the condition of salvation, but acceptance or rejection of Christ, with good works as a fruit of salvation. The *immediate result* of this testing was the rejection of Christ by the Jews, and His crucifixion by Jew and Gentile. The *predicted end* of the testing of man under grace is the apostasy of the professing church, and the resultant apocalyptic judgments." [22] The "new covenant" which is in force during this period is said to be "absolutely unconditional, and, since no responsibility is by it committed to man, it is final and irreversible." [23]

7. *Fullness of Times or the Kingdom*. This is the millennium during which the Davidic covenant is fulfilled.[24] This final dispensation "gathers into itself under Christ all past 'times.'" [25] "Upon His return the King will restore the Davidic monarchy in His own person, re-gather dispersed Israel, establish His power over all the earth, and reign one thousand years. The kingdom of heaven, thus established under David's divine Son, has for its object the restoration of the divine authority in the earth . . . "[26]

Different Ways of Salvation?

Dispensationalists have reacted vigorously to the charge that dispensations are ways of salvation, as though there was more than one way. The doctrinal statement of Dallas Theological Seminary speaks explicitly to this point when it says that "dispensations are not ways of salvation nor different methods of administering the so-called Covenant of Grace. They are not in themselves dependent on covenant relationships but are ways of life and responsibility to God which test the submission of man to His revealed will during a particular time."[27] The statement maintains further that salvation is and always has been only by grace through faith, and not by man's self-effort. Salvation has always been based on the shed blood of Christ, apart from which there is no salvation. But inasmuch as explicit faith in Christ was impossible in the ages prior to His incarnation, the faith of the Old Testament saints "was manifested in other ways as is shown by the long record in Hebrews 11:1-40. . . . Their faith thus manifested was counted unto them for righteousness." [28] Though this statement is clear in its disclaimer, and though Scofield would most likely have heartily endorsed it, one cannot escape the conclusion that his explanatory notes merit the criticism that has been made. The most that can be said for Scofield is that he is ambiguous at this point. The ambiguity grows out of his lack of clarity concerning the relation of faith to salvation. Does man's salvation in any way depend upon his response to the dispensational tests? Both Scofield and the theological statement of Dallas suggest that the answer is yes, at least in some sense. Is the nature of the response demanded in each dispensation the same? Here again both Scofield and his contemporary brethren would probably reply yes, but their dispensational distinctions, if they mean anything at all, seem to belie their answer. Scofield says that the difference between the dispensations of law and grace is that "the point of testing is no longer legal obedience as the condition of salvation, but acceptance or rejection of Christ, with good works as a fruit of salvation." [29] Or again, commenting on the prayer, "And forgive us our debts, as we forgive our debtors," he says, "Under law forgiveness is conditioned upon a like spirit in us; under grace we are forgiven for Christ's sake, and exhorted to forgive because we have been forgiven." [30] Certainly one must conclude from these statements and from others which sharply contrast the two dispensations, and thereby make the same implicit contrast, that God does employ a different approach to salvation in each dispensation. Even though certain legal relationships between Christ's death and the individual's salvation are said to apply in every dispensation, who can deny that there is a real difference in the methodology of salvation in each? If this is not the case, how is one to understand Ehlert's statement that the feature which distinguishes a dispensation from an age is its relation to God's redemptive program?

While Scofield does not discuss the relation of covenants and dispensations as such, he does differentiate between them. Covenants, he says, "condition [the] life and salvation" of mankind.[31]

Some of the covenants directly institute and define a dispensation. Thus he says concerning the covenant made with Noah that it "subjects humanity to a new test. Its distinctive feature is the institution, for the first time, of human government. . . . It follows that the third dispensation is distinctively that of human government." [32] Other covenants do not have a definitive relation to their contemporary dispensation. The Palestinian covenant (Deut. 30:3), given during the dispensation of law, merely "gives the conditions under which Israel entered the land of promise." [33] His explanation of the meaning and character of the covenant made with Abraham implies another dissimilarity between covenants and dispensations. He says that the dispensation of promise must be distinguished from the covenant of promise. "The former is a mode of testing; the latter is everlasting because unconditional." [34] His point is that while the dispensation ended with the giving of the law, the covenant continued unchanged. The implication is that while a covenant may be made in conjunction with a particular dispensation and, in a sense, define its distinctive character, yet the covenant relationship is independent of the dispensation and does not necessarily end with it. Chafer's discussion of the covenants clarifies this. He says that the Adamic covenant prescribes the conditions for man's life on earth after the fall, and that much in this covenant continues in effect until the curse is lifted from creation.[35]

Scofield's reason for cautioning the reader against a confusion between the covenant of promise and the dispensation of promise can be explained in the light of the previous discussion concerning the relation of the dispensational test to salvation. Covenants, at least some of them, have to do not only with man's life on earth but also with his salvation, while dispensations apparently do not. As a matter of fact, Scofield's eight covenants are of different sorts, conditioning both life in this world (see his statement that dispensations "condition human life on the earth") and salvation. His lack of consistency on this point makes his notes very difficult to interpret. Are we to conclude that since the Abrahamic covenant was not abrogated at Sinai, it "conditioned salvation" during the dispensation of Law? If so, what is the meaning of the careful contrasts drawn between the Mosaic covenant and the New Covenant as though they represent contrasting means of salvation? He says that the New Covenant is "efficaciously" better than the Mosaic. It is "established on 'better' (i.e. unconditional) promises." [36] Though he does not state it explicitly, much less explain it consistently, he seems to assume that the New Covenant and the covenant of promise are closely related in character and are to be sharply distinguished from all the rest. The difference is that the former are unconditional and mediate the terms of man's salvation as well as regulate his life on earth, while the latter are conditional and only define man's dispensational tests. His entire treatment lacks system and he does not follow his statements to their logical conclusion. As it stands, it is difficult to see how Scofield's defenders can expect their denial of the charge that he teaches more than one way of salvation to be taken seriously.

Scofield's Dispensationalism as a Method of Interpretation

In the course of time premillennialism became so well established in conservative circles that dispensationalism no longer functioned as an argument for it, but in the minds of many became identified with it. With Scofield the system became an end in itself, and was perfected as a complete norm of interpretation. It is now quite common for men holding to the system to argue against other interpretations that they are not according to "dispensational truth." This, of course, was Darby's conception from the beginning, but it took some time for it to be completely accepted by the men in the prophetic and Bible conference movements.

About 1900 Scofield published a book, entitled *Rightly Dividing the Word of Truth,* in which he set forth the scheme later used in his *Reference Bible.* He lists ten distinctions which must be made in order to understand Scripture. All of these are said to have "dispensational significance." There is little logical coherence in the distinctions, but they represent the interpretation of contemporary dispensationalists and are given here for that reason. They are: (1) "The Jew, the Gentile, and the Church of God." (2) "The seven dispensations." (3) "The two advents." (4) "The two resurrections"—of the saints before the millennium and of the wicked dead afterward. (5) "The five judgments." These are: The judgment of the sins of believers in the cross, of sin in the believer which results in chastisement by the Lord, of the conduct or works of believers at the time of the rapture, of living nations just before the millennium to determine who shall enter into the Kingdom, and lastly, the wicked dead at the great white throne after the millennium. (6) "Law and grace." This is the sharp distinction made between the Mosaic and Christian dispensations. Much of the difficulty in modern interpretation, it is held, is due to an improper mingling of law and grace in this dispensation. (7) "The believer's two natures." (8) "The believer's standing and state." This was a bone of contention among the earlier Plymouth Brethren. The distinction was urged by some of their leaders, and was taken over unquestioningly by Scofield. It rests on a deterministic interpretation of the doctrine of election and the "unconditional" quality of the new covenant. It is the foundation for the "eternal security" teaching. (9) "Salvation and rewards." This is a corollary of the previous distinction. (10) "Believers and professors." The Church or Christendom—"the Kingdom in a mystery"—is a mixture of good and bad. This is the meaning of the parable of the tares and of the net with all kinds of fish. True believers are the elect, the gathered-out "bride of Christ." These are saved; mere professors are lost.[37]

It is quite clear that these distinctions do not all have the same significance for interpreting Scripture. In fact, they are of such a varying character that it is almost impossible to find any system. The basic division is between Jew, Gentile, and Church. These might be thought of as genera. The Scriptures are fitted into these categories, or, to use Scofield's phraseology, applied dispensationally. For example, we are told that "last days" means one thing when it refers to Jews and quite another when it refers to the Gentiles or to the Church.[38] Or that the return of Jesus Christ has a "threefold relation: to the church, to Israel, to the nations [Gentiles]." [39] Certain books of the Bible are said to be Jewish in their character and application. The Sermon on the Mount is for the Jewish Kingdom during the millennium, and has only a "beautiful moral application to the Christian." [40] Chafer taught that the Scriptures addressed specifically to the Church are the Gospel of John (especially the Upper Room Discourses), the Acts, and the Epistles.[41]

The seven ages or dispensations furnish a kind of historical framework within which the drama unfolds. Most of the rest of the distinctive categories are merely theological tenets which are used to classify proof texts. The classification proceeds on the assumption that the words of the Bible have a uniform, literal meaning throughout. The method of approach is analytical, and the explanations or notes often consist merely of an outline arrangement of the phrases or words of the text. Minute distinctions and shades of meaning are invariably contrasted and pigeonholed separately. Scofield notes, for example, that "the kingdom of God is to be distinguished from the kingdom of heaven." [42] In his discussion of the work of the Holy Spirit the whole exposition proceeds on the assumption that the three prepositions, *in, with,* and *upon,* which are used metaphorically in Scripture to describe the Spirit's presence with God's people, denote three distinct and separate functions of the Spirit in relation to men.[43] "Rightly dividing the Scripture" means, thus, comparing and contrasting texts in the light of dispensational divisions. Historical and psychological factors are given little or no consideration.

As has been pointed out previously, one of the major problems to which the dispensationalists addressed themselves was the interpretation of God's revelation of Himself in history. They sought to maintain a concept of progressive revelation consistent with belief in the infallibility of the literal message of the Bible. It is interesting to see how this has crystallized in Scofield.

Scofield explained his concept of the unfolding of truth in an article published in 1902. He says:

> Whoever reads the Scriptures with any consecutiveness or attention cannot fail to perceive that in them may be traced a gradual unfolding of divine truth and purpose. Such a reader sees that nothing is told all at once, that nothing is done without preparation, without deliberation. . . .
>
> When this is understood, then it begins to be seen that there is a beautiful system in this gradualness of unfolding. The past is seen to fall into periods, marked off by distinct limits, and distinguishable period from period, by something peculiar to each. Thus it comes to be understood that there is a doctrine of the Ages, or Dispensations, in the Bible.[44]

He says essentially the same thing in the introduction to the *Reference Bible*. "The Dispensations are distinguished, exhibiting the majestic, progressive order of the divine dealings of God with humanity, 'the increasing purpose' which runs through and links together the ages, from the beginning of the life of man to the end in eternity." [45]

As an example of Scofield's concept of progressive revelation we may use the doctrine of the Holy Spirit, of which he says that it "follows, in common with every other doctrine, the law of progressive development."[46] He notes five "natural divisions in this progressive unfolding." They are: "1. The Holy Spirit before the Incarnation of Christ. 2. The Holy Spirit in relation to the Person and ministry of Christ from the Incarnation to Pentecost. 3. The Holy Spirit from Pentecost to the opening of the door to the Gentiles. 4. The Holy Spirit in His present offices and relationships as defined in the Epistles. 5. The Holy Spirit (prophetically) in the future kingdom age." [47] In his following discussion he says that in the Old Testament the Spirit is revealed as a "divine Person," and refers to His work in the creation and in bestowing gifts. His work in regenerating the Old Testament believers is also assumed, since they were members of the Kingdom of God and John 3:5 makes it clear that no man can see the Kingdom of God except he be born of the Spirit. This provides background for, and remains unchanged in, the New Testament. But in two particulars there is a difference between the work of the Spirit in the Old Testament and the New Testament. First, the Old Testament saints did not have "the indwelling Spirit of sonship, . . . Even a sincere believer had no assurance that the Spirit might not forsake him (Psalm 51:11); whereas the believer of this dispensation has an express promise of the abiding of the Spirit." Second, "All the offices of the Spirit were reserved within the sovereign will of God." [48] The Old Testament saints had no way revealed to them by which they might receive the Spirit. This was changed during Christ's ministry when He told the disciples that they might receive the Spirit by prayer. This "astonishing" privilege was too great for their faith, so they did not ask or receive. Because of this failure on their part, Christ toward the end of His ministry promised to ask for them. Further, Christ defined the coming ministry of the Spirit in a threefold way; namely, as a dwelling *with,* a being *in,* and a coming *upon* believers. "The coming One [Holy Spirit] should be 'with' men, convicting, converting, regenerating; 'within' men, as a fountain of living water, cleansing, renewing, satisfying; 'upon' men, bestowing gifts and power for service." [49] The fulfillment of this began immediately after the resurrection when Jesus breathed on the disciples and the Holy Spirit came to dwell *in* them. It was completed on Pentecost when He came *upon* them. In another sense, however, the process was not completed until the conversion of Cornelius when the Spirit came upon the Gentiles without *any human intervention* such as prayer or laying on of hands. This marks a clean break with the transition period—which is Jewish in character—as it is portrayed in the early chapters of Acts. Scofield explains that Acts 11:44 is "one of the pivotal points of Scripture. Heretofore the Gospel has been offered to Jews only, and the Holy Spirit bestowed upon believing Jews through apostolic mediation. But now the normal order for this age is reached: the Holy Spirit is given without delay, mediation, or other condition than simple faith in Jesus Christ." [50] He says that the "impartation of the Spirit as indwelling the believer simply and only because he was a believer, marked the tremendous transition from the age of law to the age of Grace." [51]

Aside from the fact that Scofield has omitted much relevant data which materially affects his interpretation, and in some cases has drawn dubious implications from references in order to support his interpretation, what can be said for his idea of progressive development? Even cursory observation reveals that there are actually only three steps in the development, though his fondness for a seven-point outline somewhat obscures this in the *Reference Bible*. These three stages are (1) the doctrine under the law dispensation, (2) the transition during the ministry of Christ and the early ministry of the apostles, and (3) the full-blown doctrine under the dispensation of grace. The one essential development, as he himself states, is the dispensational one from a more or less erratic movement of the Spirit upon men to the abiding presence of the Spirit in the believer "simply because he is a believer." This involves not so much a progressive revelation based upon and fulfilling a previous revelation as a dispensational difference in the mode of the Spirit's operation. One notes further that there is no mention of any development of the doctrine within the Old Testament itself. It springs like Athena, as it were, full-armed from the head of Zeus. In fact, a trinitarian understanding of the Holy Spirit as a divine person seems to be assumed for the Old Testament. As for the transition period, which is allegedly portrayed in the Gospels and early chapters of Acts, one can only say that the developments cited lack coherence and historical relatedness. Scofield does not reckon with the fact that three of the Gospels were written after most of the Epistles and may reflect interpretations of the Holy Spirit's character and work which represent a final rather than a transitional state in the development of the doctrine. Thus, while his initial observations are correct, his interpretation of the data into a series of transitional steps is open to serious question. Again let it be noted that for Scofield the "law of progressive development" does not represent a growing enlightenment and understanding as man grasps the proffered revelation of God. Rather, it represents modal changes in the Holy Spirit's dealings with mankind.

It is in the dispensations themselves that Scofield claims to be able to distinguish progressive revelation and a gradual unfolding of divine truth. However, an examination of his outline and explanations makes it abundantly evident that he is only paying lip service to the concept of progress in revelation. We have already noted that by definition a dispensation has no essential connection with a time period or age, and that, in fact, the relation between the two is rather complex, with dispensations continuing through several ages and often overlapping one another. They do not follow one another in a progressive or organically related fashion. They do not in any significant or genuinely historical sense prepare for those which follow or grow out of those which precede them. What meaningful continuity is there between the dispensation of conscience and that of government? Or what progress in the revelation of the plan of redemption is to be noted? The dispensational changes are imposed from the outside and have little or no connection to any historical act. This lack of historical relatedness is most strikingly seen in the fact that the two dispensations of law and grace, which form the major content of the Bible, are injected as two parentheses between the giving and the fulfilling of the promised Kingdom. The law is "intermediary discipline." The Church is a parenthetic stopgap until the Kingdom is brought in by a cataclysmic intervention.

The final answer of the dispensationalist to the problem of development in history seems to be an implicit denial of the possibility of progress, claims to the contrary notwithstanding. Reacting against a false optimism and the assumption of inevitable evolutionary progress, dispensationalism reverted to an equally pagan concept of history which denies the possibility of progress and asserts the inevitability of futility on the historical level. The philosophy of history presented is essentially the Greek concept of cycles, each cycle ending in apostasy and judgment. God is not represented as working out His plan *in the historical process,* but as appearing intermittently, as it were, to begin a new cycle by supernatural intervention.

Postponement Theory

Scofield's statements concerning the nature and task of the Church are essentially the same as those of his predecessors. He distinguishes between the true Church and Christendom; between the New Testament Church and the Old Testament Church. These latter two have only the name *ekklesia* in common. "All else is contrast." [52] He also makes a fundamental distinction between the Kingdom in its present manifestation ("the mystery form of the Kingdom") and the Church. The purpose of the Church is to "call out" from the nations a people of God. Scofield's contribution does not lie so much in his definition of doctrine as in the more intangible area of attitude or mood. He is more consistently and intensely pessimistic about the organized church than his teacher, J. H. Brookes, and in this he is nearer to Darby and Kelly. It is quite evident that the writings of the Plymouth Brethren set the mood as well as the theological basis for his position. He read these men at a time when liberalism and secularism were growing in the American churches, and their leaven worked rapidly and well. Besides this, we must remember that Scofield himself had never known loyalty to a denominational tradition. He was converted by a Y.M.C.A. worker, joined a Congregational church at the age of thirty-six, and almost from the beginning of his ministry spent a great deal of his time in interdenominational evangelistic and Bible conference work. This orientation made Scofield much more ready to accept uncritically the writings of the Plymouth Brethren than his predecessors had been.

In the area of doctrine Scofield moved beyond his immediate predecessors toward a more consistent Plymouth Brethren position. He made his contribution to dispensational doctrine by adding further analytical details to the system that was already worked out. His development of the so-called postponement theory of the Kingdom is a good example.

It is true that J. H. Brookes and others who leaned toward dispensationalism in the early years of the prophetic conference movement held that the Kingdom had been postponed. W. E.

Blackstone was perhaps the most uncritical in his acceptance of the doctrine. Even men like Nathaniel West considered the Church parenthetic, but only in the sense that it was not revealed explicitly to the Old Testament prophets. West held that the Kingdom was, in a limited sense, already here waiting for its final perfection in the millennium after Christ's coming. And while some were inclined to make a sharper dispensational break than West did, on the whole they did concede that there is continuity between the Church and the Kingdom. In Scofield the dichotomy between Church and Kingdom is complete.

Historically, the concepts of the postponement of the Kingdom and the parenthetic character of the Church, as they are fully developed in Scofield, derive from two sources—one premillennial and the other dispensational. By the time they were introduced into America by the Plymouth Brethren, however, they were fully integrated into one doctrine. The assumption which underlies both of these approaches is the necessity for a literal fulfillment of all the prophetic language of the Old Testament. Beginning with this premise, historic premillennialism supplied the concept of a parenthetic time period. By this was meant that the Old Testament prophets had a foreshortened view of future events and did not perceive the period of the Church's formation and work between the two advents of Christ. They spoke in their prophecies as though the final Kingdom would be immediately established by the Messiah at His first advent. Thus the parenthetic character of the Church did not necessarily mean that it had no historical relationship to the Kingdom. Neither did it necessarily imply that Christ did not intend to establish the Church from the beginning of His ministry. West could even use the phrase "evolution of the Kingdom," and he with other premillennialists insisted that the Kingdom is now partially present in the Church.

The dispensational approach emphasized the absolute cleavage between the Kingdom and the Church as entirely separate entities. The Kingdom is a distinctly Jewish phenomenon. It was promised to the Jews in the Old Testament, and Christ came as the Jewish Messiah to fulfill this promise. He did not intend in the first instance to establish the Church, but when it became clear that the Jews would not accept Him as their Messiah he began to prepare His disciples for this new thing which would be brought into being. According to this teaching, Jesus Himself did not found the Church. It is the creation of the Holy Spirit and came into being for the first time on the day of Pentecost. But what of the Kingdom? Will it find its fulfillment in the Church? Or has it been dropped from God's plan because the Jews rejected their Messiah? Neither; rather the Kingdom has been postponed. William Kelly had described it thus:

> Israel did not receive the testimony of the kingdom; an entire change comes in, and the kingdom of heaven, in outward establishment, remains in suspension. The calling of God now to the Gentiles comes in as a vast parenthesis between this message to the lost sheep in Israel and its full accomplishment in the last days.[53]

Scofield combined these two concepts, as Darby and Kelly before him, into a blend which accentuates the dispensational cleavage and defines clearly the postponement of the Kingdom. He says that Jesus, after being rejected by the Jewish leaders about midway in His career, changed His message and no longer offered the Kingdom to the Jewish nation. From this point on He is said to have offered "rest" and "service" to individuals who recognized their need, and to have prepared His disciples for His coming death and resurrection. He did make a prophetic reference to the Church toward the end of His ministry, but never made known the mystery of the Church. He worked to the end of His life as a Jew in the Law dispensation. The early chapters of Acts portray a transition period in which the Jews were called into the Church, and the normal order of the age was not reached until the time of the conversion of Cornelius. The mystery of the Church was revealed through Paul in the Epistles.

Scofield's significance in American dispensationalism lies in the fact that he sought to put the more tenuous theological concepts into concrete outline form. Scofield, the lawyer, is at work building the case from the mass of evidence. He is not working out solutions to vital problems. Rather, he is arranging the solutions which were already worked out into a cogent, forceful argument. One might almost say that he is a dispensationalist for the sake of the system. This gives his work a certain mechanical quality and lack of vitality. If we ask whether he represents a development in dispensationalism which is vital to the larger theological picture, the answer is no. He represents, rather, the system turned in upon itself. He offers nothing of positive significance. His predecessors were the innovators, the radicals; he has become the conservative, the scholastic.

A Concluding Word

Many conservative writers have called dispensationalism a heresy. George E. Ladd feels that heresy is too strong a word, however, and pleads for tolerance of the position within the Church. But are the issues limited to minor differences in the ordering of future events? Certainly we will all agree that many men of outstanding piety and zeal have espoused dispensational beliefs. In the mind of the author, however, the issues which are raised by dispensationalism are crucial for the life of the Church and the understanding of the Scriptures. Perhaps a concluding word of evaluation will be helpful in pointing up the issues.

If there is any one word which can be used to describe the dispensationalist's approach to the Bible, it is the word literalism. The term is not only leveled as a criticism by those opposing the movement, but is accepted as a virtue by those within the movement. Because of this, it is necessary to define more carefully what the term means. The dispensationalists themselves often use the word to mean grammatical in contrast to allegorical. Thus they strongly defend the grammatico-historical method of interpretation. But they carry this a step further when they insist on the unconditional literal fulfillment of all the promises of a material, earthly kingdom in exactly the same sense that the Old Testament saints might have expected. Obviously, the modern critics of dispensationalism's literalistic approach to Scripture are not suggesting that the allegorical method is to be preferred to the grammatico-historical method of exegesis. And neither are the conservative critics suggesting that God will not fulfill His promises which He has made through the prophets, though some of the liberal critics do mean this. On the other hand, it is also obvious that the dispensationalists cannot claim that all of their interpretations are strictly literal. Their writings yield striking examples of typology which sometimes borders on allegory. What, then, is the real nature of this criticism?

The dispensationalist interpretation is built on an inadequate concept of the nature of language and its use. In seeking to uphold the supernatural quality of the Biblical narrative it has assumed that the Biblical language is like the language of a science textbook; that is, that its terms have a fixed meaning from beginning to end. Recently one of the most distinguished scholars in the dispensationalist school stated that there is no essential difference between the language of the Bible and a medical dictionary. On the basis of this assumption they proceed to exegete the Scripture without giving adequate attention to the historical and psychological context. Consequently, their system is like a mosaic made up of particles taken from here and there in the Bible and fitted into the picture at the will of the designer. Or, to change the figure, they approach the Bible as though it were a great mosaic which can be understood only by dissecting its elemental particles and reclassifying them according to their size and color. Their norm is mechanical and schematic, and minimizes too much the human element in Scripture. Unwittingly perhaps, they have foisted upon the Bible their own assumptions and have on the basis of these assumptions read out of the Bible their own dispensational distinctions. It is very easy to demonstrate that even the word *oikonomia,* translated "dispensation" in the New Testament, does not mean what they interpret it to mean.

Perhaps an even more serious question is raised by the dispensationalist teaching that certain parts of the Bible apply almost exclusively to national Israel and not to Christians. It has been the deep conviction of the Church from its beginning that the whole Bible, including the Old Testament, is the Christian's book and speaks of Christ. In fact, this conviction was used by the early Church to justify the allegorical method of interpreting the Bible. It is obvious on the surface that not all of the passages of the Old Testament have immediate devotional or practical value for the lives of Christians if they are given merely a grammatical and historical interpretation. There is little devotional value in the genealogical tables, for example. Early Christian teachers, however, felt that every passage should have such immediate value, and in order to make them yield such instruction they allegorized their message. While we do not share these early teachers' enthusiasm for allegory, we do recognize that their concern to relate the whole Bible to the life of the Church was valid.

Ever since the time of the Apostle Paul it has been the general understanding of Christians that there are different kinds of commands and instructions in the Old Testament and that not all of them apply directly to the Church. None of us would try to regulate our lives by all of the laws given in Exodus 21-23. The very concept of progressive revelation implies that there will be elements in the earlier revelation which may be outmoded and superseded by later revelation. Thus the Old Testament has been conceived as a *preparation* for Christ and His Church. But dispensationalism goes further than this and practically denies that the Old Testament has any relation to the Church at all. It teaches that the Church is not visualized in the Old Testament; that there is no historical relation between the people of God under the Old Covenant and the New; that the major part of the Old Testament revelation is *law* which is diametrically opposed to the revelation of grace in the Epistles of the New Testament. The Old Testament is a Jewish book for Israel under the Old Covenant and under the millennial covenant yet to come. Thus the Old Testament prophecies have no reference at all to the Church and no fulfillment through it.

This dispensational distinction is pressed even further, so that Jesus' life and teachings are lost to the Church. Jesus is said to have lived and taught as a Jew under the dispensation of law. Indeed, He is not the founder of the Church. In His teachings He was offering the Kingdom to the Jews; therefore His teachings do not have any direct application to the life of the Church. They represent law, and the Church is living under grace. Scofield does admit that the Sermon on the Mount has "beautiful moral application" to the Christian life, but its immediate point of reference is the Jewish Kingdom which is to be established during the millennium. Here, interestingly enough, the old question of Jesus versus Paul meets us in new guise, and according to the dispensational solution the Church must be satisfied with Paul. The New Testament writings which are directed to the Church are the Epistles and certain passages from the Gospel of John. And we are told that until one recognizes these distinctions the Bible will not yield its vast store of treasure. Whether or not one uses the term heresy to describe this kind of teaching, it can hardly be denied that the dispensational solution of this difficult problem is sharply divergent from the general consensus of the Church throughout the ages.

We have already considered at some length the dispensational concept of the Church and its task, so a brief word in conclusion will suffice.

According to dispensational teaching the Church is a spiritual fellowship of those who have been called to participation in Christ. Its visible boundaries cannot be discerned by man. It has no organizational structure. It is, to use Darby's words, a "heavenly body." It is to be carefully distinguished from Christendom or the organized church. There is a very sound element in this emphasis upon the spiritual quality of the Church's life, but when it is emphasized so exclusively that the reality of the Church's earthly existence is denied, great harm can result. It is a matter of record that the denomination which has been most closely associated with the dispensational movement has been torn with division and strife almost from the beginning. It is also a matter of record that many ardent Christians who have espoused the doctrine have been lost to their denominational mission program. This is not mere coincidence. Emphasis upon the strictly spiritual character of the Church has led dispensationalists to frown upon all attempts at unity which begin with the recognition of the existing denominational structures. Members of existing denominations were encouraged to come out of apostate Christendom into the true body of Christ and there find spiritual fellowship in testimony and praise and evangelistic activity.

In keeping with its definition of the nature of the Church, dispensationalism has also circumscribed its task. The Church's work is to call out a bride for Christ, to prepare men and women for a heavenly existence. It is not concerned with the life of the Church in this world as such. Much less is it to be concerned with the world. Men's souls are to be prepared to escape the judgment which will come upon the world. This understanding of the nature and task of the Church has led those who adhere to this teaching to think of missionary witness almost solely in terms of preaching. One group strongly influenced by this doctrine established a mission in an area where there were thousands of refugees who were in dire need of food and clothing. They refused, however, to be involved in any ministry of relief to these people because their job was simply to preach the gospel. Furthermore, they were critical of those Christians who sought earnestly to combine relief and preaching in a spiritual ministry to them. Here again there is an essential element of truth. Christians are to be concerned with the spiritual life of their fellows. We certainly believe that the spiritual underlies and conditions all of life in this world and the next. But exclusive emphasis upon this aspect of our existence leaves us with a truncated gospel. Jesus Christ was concerned with the whole man. He fed the hungry, gave sight to the blind, healed the sick, and preached the good news to the poor. We believe that in this Jesus is to be our example, dispensational distinctions notwithstanding.

Dispensationalist eschatology has also colored the concept of the Church's ministry to the world. The Church is not vitally related to the processes of history. It is a parenthesis in God's plan for the human race, not a step forward toward the culmination of God's purposes in history. Furthermore, the Church is impotent to change the course of this age. Dispensations follow their own invariable pattern, ending in ruin and judgment. This minimizes the place of the Church in God's plan for the ages. We miss completely the Pauline exaltation of the Church as the great fulfillment and glorious continuation of the work which God began with Abraham. They have bypassed Paul's concept of the Church as being the "fulness of Christ," completing His mission through the power and guidance of the Holy Spirit.

Dispensationalism has been a reactionary movement from its inception. It sought to maintain the *status quo* during a period of change. It frankly attempted to redefine certain traditional theological concepts in order to strengthen its position against liberalizing tendencies. It represented a position so diametrically opposed to the incipient liberalism that it could even suggest that traditional conservatism was in some areas compromising with the new developments. This strongly reactionary character has laid it open to the charge of escapism and obscurantism. But to dismiss the movement as escapist—"a phase of wartime thinking"—is to forget that it had its inception and an initial period of remarkable growth during one of the most optimistic eras of American history. That it was obscurantist in the sense that it failed to understand and grapple satisfactorily with the real issues of the day is more admissible. It must also be admitted that the leaders of the movement made only feeble attempts to understand the issues. They readily accepted the reports of the sensational newspapers which opposed the new ideas, and they often accused their opponents of conclusions which they did not actually draw. By and large the movement has maintained the same characteristics to this day. It has strengthened its scholarship and systematized its position, but it has shown little inclination to profit from its criticism.

Bibliography

A. Primary Sources

1. BOOKS

Blackstone, W. E., *Jesus Is Coming*, 2nd ed. New York: Fleming H. Revell, 1886.

Brookes, J. H., *Maranatha: or, The Lord Cometh*, 5th ed. New York: E. Brendell, 1878.

Cameron, Robert, *Scriptural Truth About the Lord's Return*. New York: Fleming H. Revell, 1922.

Chafer, Lewis Sperry, *He That Is Spiritual*. New York: Our Hope Publishing Co., 1918.

Chafer, Lewis Sperry, *Systematic Theology*, Vol. I-VIII. Dallas, Texas: Dallas Seminary Press, 1948.

Duffield, George, *Dissertations on the Prophecies Relative to the Second Coming of Jesus Christ*. New York: Dayton and Newman, 1842.

Gaebelein, Arno C., *Half A Century, The Autobiography of A Servant*. New York: Our Hope Publishing Co., 1930.

Gaebelein, Arno C., *The Harmony of the Prophetic Word*. New York: Fleming H. Revell, 1907.

Gaebelein, Arno C., *The History of the Scofield Reference Bible*. New York: Our Hope Publishing Co., 1943.

Kellogg, S. H., *The Jews: or, Prediction and Fulfillment an Argument for the Times*. New York: Anson D. F. Randolph and Co., 1883.

Kelly, William, *Lectures on the Gospel of Matthew*, 5th ed. New York: Loizeaux Brothers, 1943. (First edition, London, 1868.)

Mackintosh, C. H., *Papers on the Lord's Coming*. Chicago: The Bible Institute Colportage Association (n.d.).

Morgan, G. Campbell, *God's Methods With Man*, In Time: Past, Present and Future. New York: Fleming H. Revell, 1898.

Munhall, *The Lord's Return and Kindred Truth*. Chicago: Fleming H. Revell, 1885.

Needham, George, editor, *Prophetic Studies of the International Prophetic Conference* (1886). Chicago: Fleming H. Revell, 1886.

Scofield, C. I., *Plain Papers on the Doctrine of the Holy Spirit*. New York: Fleming H. Revell, 1899.

Scofield, C. I., editor, *The Scofield Reference Bible*. New York: Oxford University Press, 1909.

Scofield, C. I., *Rightly Dividing the Word of Truth*, Being Ten Outline Studies of the More Important Divisions of Scripture. New York: Loizeaux Brothers (n.d.).

Trotter, William, *Plain Papers on Prophetic and Other Subjects*, 2nd ed. London: William Mackintosh (n.d.—written c. 1863).

West, Nathaniel, *The Apostle Paul and the Any-Moment Rapture Theory*. Philadelphia: J. H. Armstrong (printer), 1893.

West, Nathaniel, *The Coming of the Lord in the "Teaching of the Twelve Apostles."* Philadelphia: J. H. Armstrong (printer), 1892.

West, Nathaniel, editor, *Premillennial Essays of the Prophetic Conference* (1878). Chicago: Fleming H. Revell, 1879.

West, Nathaniel, *The Thousand Years in Both Testaments (Studies in Eschatology)*. New York: Fleming H. Revell, 1880.

2. PERIODICALS

Bibliotheca Sacra (1934-   ), Dallas Theological Seminary.

The Truth (1875-1897), James H. Brookes, editor.

The Watchword (1878-1897), A. J. Gordon, editor.

Our Hope (1894-   ), Arno C. Gaebelein, editor.

The Watchword and Truth (1898-1921), Robert Cameron, editor.

Waymarks in the Wilderness, and Scriptural Guide (1864-1872), James Inglis, editor.

B. Secondary Sources

1. BOOKS

Allis, O. T., *Prophecy and the Church*, An Examination of the Claim of Dispensationalists That the Christian Church Is a Mystery Parenthesis. Philadelphia: Presbyterian and Reformed Publishing Co., 1945.

Berry, George Ricker, *Premillennialism and Old Testament Prediction*, A Study in Interpretation. Chicago: University of Chicago Press, 1929.

Case, Shirley Jackson, *The Millennial Hope, A Phase of War-Time Thinking*. Chicago: University of Chicago Press, 1918.

Cole, Stewart G., *The History of Fundamentalism*. New York: Richard R. Smith, Inc., 1931.

Hamilton, Floyd E., *The Basis of Millennial Faith*. Grand Rapids: Wm. B. Eerdmans Publishing Co., 1942.

Hodges, Jesse Wilson, *Christ's Kingdom and Coming*. Grand Rapids: Wm. B. Eerdmans Publishing Co., 1957.

Ironside, H. A., *A Historical Sketch of the Brethren Movement*, An Account of Its Inception, Progress, Principles and Failures, and Its Lessons for Present-day Believers. Grand Rapids: Zondervan Publishing House, 1942.

Kromminga, D. H., *The Millennium in the Church*, Studies in the History of Christian Chiliasm. Grand Rapids: Wm. B. Eerdmans Publishing Co., 1945.

La Sor, William S., *A Study of the Exegetical Basis of Premillennialism*. A master's thesis at Princeton Seminary (typed), 1942.

Ladd, George E., *Crucial Questions About the Kingdom of God*. Grand Rapids: Wm. B. Eerdmans Publishing Co., 1952.

Ladd, George E., *The Blessed Hope*. Grand Rapids: Wm. B. Eerdmans Publishing Co., 1956.

Mauro, Philip, *The Gospel of the Kingdom, With an Examination of Modern Dispensationalism*. Boston: Hamilton Bros., 1928.

Murray, George L., *Millennial Studies, A Search for Truth*. Grand Rapids: Baker Book House, 1948.

Neatby, W. Blair, *A History of the Plymouth Brethren*, 2nd ed. London: Hodder & Stoughton, 1902.

Rall, Harris Franklin, *Modern Premillennialism and the Christian Hope*. New York: Abingdon Press, 1920.

Reese, Alexander, *The Approaching Advent of Christ*, An Examination of the Teaching of J. N. Darby and His Followers. London: Marshall, Morgan and Scott, 1937.

Rutgers, William H., *Premillennialism in America*. Goes, Holland: Oosterbaan and Le Gointre, 1930.

Sheldon, Henry C., *Studies in Recent Adventism*. New York: Abingdon Press, 1915.

Snowden, James H., *The Coming of the Lord: Will It Be Premillennial?* New York: The Macmillan Company, 1919.

Sweet, W. W., *The Story of Religion in America*. New York: Harper & Brothers, 1950.

Turner, W. G., *John Nelson Darby*. London: C. A. Hammond, 1944.

2. ARTICLES AND TRACTS

Allis, O. T., "Modern Dispensationalism and the Doctrine of the Unity of the Scriptures," *Evangelical Quarterly*, January, 1936.

Bear, James E., "Dispensationalism and the Covenant of Grace," *Union Seminary Review* (Richmond), Vol. XLIV, 1938, pp. 285-307.

Bear, James E., "Historic Premillennialism," *Union Seminary Review*, Vol. LV, 1944, pp. 193-221.

Boase, S. C., "Darby, John Nelson," *Dictionary of National Biography,* Vol. XIV. New York: The Macmillan Company, 1888, pp. 43-44.

Bowman, John Wick, "Dispensationalism," *Interpretation,* Vol. X, 1956, pp. 170-187.

Briggs, C. A., "Origin and History of Premillennialism," *Lutheran Quarterly Review,* Vol. IX, 1879, pp. 207-245.

Ehlert, Arnold D., "A Bibliography of Dispensationalism," *Bibliotheca Sacra,* Vol. CI, CII, CIII (in series), 1944-1946.

McConnell, Francis J., "The Causes of Premillennialism," *Harvard Theological Review,* Vol. XII, 1919, pp. 179-192.

Pieters, Albertus, *A Candid Examination of the Scofield Bible,* Swengel, Pa.: Bible Truth Depot, 1938.

Notes and Acknowledgments

Introduction

1. C. H. Hopkins, *The Rise of the Social Gospel in American Protestantism, 1865-1915*, p. 19. Yale University Press, 1950. Used by permission.
2. Alexander Reese, *The Approaching Advent of Christ,* An Examination of the Teachings of J. N. Darby and His Followers, p. 19. Marshall, Morgan and Scott, 1937. Used by permission.
3. Lewis Sperry Chafer, "Dispensationalism," *Bibliotheca Sacra,* Vol. XCIII, 1936, pp. 392-393. Used by permission.

Chapter 1

Patterns for the Ages

1. St. Irenaeus, *The Proof of Apostolic Preaching,* sections 41, 47. The Newman Press, 1952. Used by permission.
2. *Ibid.,* section 48.
3. Arnold Ehlert, "A Bibliography of Dispensationalism," *Bibliotheca Sacra,* Vol. CII, 1945, p. 84. Used by permission.
4. See James Westfall Thompson, *A History of Historical Writing,* Vol. I, p. 527. The Macmillan Company, 1942.
5. Quoted in W. G. Turner, *John Nelson Darby,* p. 17. C. A. Hammond, 1944. Used by permission.
6. *Ibid.,* p. 18.
7. *Ibid.,* p. 8.
8. See W. Blair Neatby, *A History of the Plymouth Brethren,* 2nd edition, pp. 87 ff. Hodder & Stoughton, 1902.
9. James E. Bear, "Historic Premillennialism," *Union Seminary Review,* Vol. LV, May, 1944, p. 215. Used by permission of *Interpretation,* successor to *Union Seminary Review.*
10. Neatby, *op. cit.,* pp. 38-39. Quoting Stokes, "John Nelson Darby," *Contemporary Review,* October, 1885.
11. Ehlert, *op. cit.,* p. 87.

12. *Ibid.*, footnote to p. 87.

13. *Ibid.*, pp. 86-87. Quoting *The Collected Writings of J. N. Darby.*

14. Ehlert, *op. cit.*, p. 216.

15. A. C. Coxe, II, *Ante-Nicene Fathers,* p. 477. (Arrangement altered slightly.) Buffalo: The Christian Literature Publishing Co., 1885.

16. Ehlert, *op. cit.*, p. 217.

17. Henry M. Parsons, "The Present Age and Development of Anti-Christ," *Premillennial Essays of the Prophetic Conference* (1878), edited by Nathaniel West, p. 205. Fleming H. Revell, 1879.

18. See further discussion of this point in chapter 5.

19. *The Truth,* Vol. XI, 1885, pp. 460-466. (Arrangement altered slightly.)

20. I have not been able to check this back to the first edition, but the testimony that his diagram of the ages (which is also included in his book) was used at the Prophetic Conference in 1878 indicates clearly that he held substantially the same views then. The chart gives the substance of the outline.

21. W. E. Blackstone, *Jesus Is Coming,* 2nd edition, p. 157. Fleming H. Revell (n.d.).

22. *Ibid.*, p. 158.

23. *Ibid.*, p. 162.

24. A. J. Frost, "Condition of the Church and World at Christ's Second Advent; or, Are the Church and World to Grow Better or Worse Until He Come?", *Prophetic Studies of the International Prophetic Conference* (1886), edited by George Needham, pp. 166-168. Fleming H. Revell, 1886.

25. *Ibid.*, p. 166.

26. Robert Cameron, "The Late Jas. H. Brookes, D.D.," *The Watchword,* Vol. XIX, May, 1897, p. 115.

27. *The Truth,* Vol. XXIII, May, 1897, n.p.

28. *Ibid.*

29. J. H. Brookes, *Maranatha: or, The Lord Cometh,* 3rd edition, p. 285. (Italics mine.) New York: E. Brendell, 1874.

30. This is adapted from Brookes' discussion in *Maranatha.* Bayne's outline was published in an article entitled "The Dispensations, Prophetically and Doctrinally Considered." The dispensations are eight in number and are very clearly defined as follows:

    THE FIRST DISPENSATION we may call *the Eden dispensation.* The account of it begins at Gen. i. 24, with the creation of man on the sixth day, and concludes at Gen. iii. 24, with the placing of the cherubim on the east of Eden to keep the way of the tree of life.

    THE SECOND DISPENSATION is *the Antediluvian.* The account of it begins at Gen. iv. 4, with the birth of Cain, and concludes at Gen. viii. 14, with the drying up of the earth.

THE THIRD DISPENSATION is *the Patriarchal*. The account of it begins at Gen. viii. 15, with Noah's departure from the Ark, and concludes at Gen. l. 26, with the death of Joseph.

THE FOURTH DISPENSATION, *the Mosaic,* begins with the oppression of Israel under Pharaoh, and concludes with the birth of John the Baptist.

THE FIFTH DISPENSATION is *the Messianic,* which extends from the birth of Jesus Christ to the ascension.

THE SIXTH DISPENSATION is *the dispensation of the Holy Ghost,* or, as we sometimes call it, *the Gospel dispensation,* which extends from the day of Pentecost to the time of the gathering together of the saints under Christ in the air at His coming.

THE SEVENTH DISPENSATION is *the Millennial,* and extends from the second coming of our Lord Jesus Christ to the judgment of the Great White Throne.

THE EIGHTH DISPENSATION is *the eternal state,* when the New Jerusalem descends to the new earth, and the Tabernacle of God is with men. (*Waymarks in the Wilderness, and Scriptural Guide,* Vol. I, James Inglis ed., 1864, pp. 446-447.)

31. *Ibid.,* pp. 285-286.
32. Clouser, G. B. M., *Dispensations and Ages of Scripture. A Study of the Divine Plan for the "Age Times,"* p. 14. New York: Francis E. Fitch, 1903. Quoted from Ehlert, "A Bibliography of Dispensationalism," *Bibliotheca Sacra,* Vol. CII, 1945, p. 331. Used by permission.
33. *Ibid.,* pp. 330-331.
34. Brookes, *op. cit.,* p. 428.
35. *Ibid.,* p. 539.
36. *Ibid.,* p. 402.
37. *Ibid.,* pp. 254-255.
38. Blackstone, *op. cit.,* p. 58.
39. *The Truth,* Vol. IV, 1878, pp. 297 ff.
40. Brookes, *op. cit.,* p. 424.
41. George E. Ladd, *The Blessed Hope,* p. 54. Wm. B. Eerdmans Publishing Co., 1956.
42. G. Campbell Morgan, *God's Methods With Man,* In Time: Past, Present and Future. (Adapted.) Fleming H. Revell, 1898.
43. See John Wick Bowman, "Dispensationalism," *Interpretation,* Vol. X, 1956, pp. 174 ff.

Chapter 2

The Leaven of the Plymouth Brethren

1. George E. Ladd, *Crucial Questions About the Kingdom of God,* p. 49, footnote. Wm. B. Eerdmans Publishing Co., 1952. Used by permission.
2. Robert Cameron, "Prophetic Teachers," *The Watchword,* Vol. XVIII, October, 1896, p. 258.
3. *Dictionary of National Biography,* Vol. XIV, p. 44. The Macmillan Company, 1888.
4. W. G. Turner, *John Nelson Darby,* p. 19.
5. H. A. Ironside, *A Historical Sketch of the Brethren Movement,* p. 73. Zondervan Publishing House, 1942. Used by permission.
6. *Ibid.,* p. 196.
7. *The Truth,* Vol. XXIII, May, 1897, pp. 256-257.
8. Ironside, *op. cit.,* p. 199.
9. Turner, *op. cit.,* p. 22.
10. Quoted in Ironside, *op. cit.,* p. 197.
11. See Alexander Reese, *The Approaching Advent of Christ,* p. 19. Reese lists the four pioneer, original writers for dispensationalism as follows:
    Darby, *Lectures on the Second Coming*
            Notes on the Apocalypse
    Kelly, *Lectures on the Second Coming and Kingdom of the Lord Jesus Christ*
            Christ's Coming Again
            Lectures on the Book of Revelation
    Trotter, *Plain Papers on Prophetic and Other Subjects*
    C. H. Mackintosh, *Papers on the Lord's Coming*
12. Cameron, "Prophetic Teachers," *The Watchword,* Vol. XVIII, October, 1896, pp. 258-259. (Italics mine.)
13. W. Blair Neatby, *A History of the Plymouth Brethren,* p. 262.
14. *Ibid.,* p. 229.
15. See E. E. Whitfield, "Mackintosh, C. H.," *The New Schaff-Herzog Encyclopedia of Religious Knowledge,* Vol. VII, p. 116. Funk and Wagnalls, 1910.
16. C. H. M. (C. H. Mackintosh), *Papers on the Lord's Coming,* p. 60. The Bible Institute Colportage Association (n.d.).
17. *Ibid.,* p. 115.
18. *Ibid.,* pp. 80-81.
19. In a footnote on p. 24, Trotter says that Paper number 2 was writ-

ten in 1853, and adds, "Now, as these words are being penned, the Northern and Southern States of the once gigantic American Union are waging deadly strife with one another." In the Preface he says, "Upwards of ten years have elapsed since the first edition began." Thus the second edition can be dated sometime between 1862 and 1864.

20. William Trotter, *Plain Papers on Prophetic and Other Subjects,* 2nd edition, pp. 397 ff. (Italics mine.) London: William Mackintosh (n.d.).
21. *Ibid.,* p. 541.
22. *Ibid.,* p. 109.
23. *Ibid.,* p. 539.
24. *Ibid.,* p. 543.
25. *Ibid.,* pp. 73 ff.
26. Arno C. Gaebelein, *Half a Century, The Autobiography of a Servant,* p. 81. Our Hope Publishing Co., 1930. Used by permission.

Chapter 3

The Dispensational Norm

1. *Westminster Confession of Faith,* Chapter VII, Paragraph VI. The Presbyterian Church in the United States, revised edition, 1948.
2. George E. Ladd, *Crucial Questions About the Kingdom of God,* p. 49 fn. See also James E. Bear, "Dispensationalism and the Covenant of Grace," *Union Seminary Review,* July, 1938, pp. 285-307, for an excellent discussion of this point.
3. S. H. Kellogg, "Premillennialism," *Bibliotheca Sacra,* Vol. XLV, 1888, pp. 253-254. Used by permission. Samuel Henry Kellogg (1839-1898) was educated at Princeton University and Princeton Seminary, graduating from the Seminary in 1864. He served as a missionary in India. Later in the U. S. he was pastor of the Third Presbyterian Church, Pittsburgh, and still later he succeeded A. A. Hodge as professor of Systematic Theology at Western Seminary at Allegheny, Pa. He resigned of his own choice because his premillennialism was not in accord with the position of the Seminary. In 1892 he went back to India, where he worked until his death.
4. See chapter 4, "The Believers' Meeting for Bible Study," pp. 71, for further description of the statement.
5. *The Truth,* Vol. IV, 1878, pp. 452 ff.
6. Lewis Sperry Chafer, *He That Is Spiritual,* p. 29. Copyright by L. S. Chafer, 1918.

7. "Notes By the Way," *The Truth,* Vol. XXIII, May, 1897, p. 243.
8. A. J. Frost, "Condition of the Church and World at Christ's Second Advent," *Prophetic Studies,* p. 169.
9. A. T. Pierson, "Premillennial Motives to Evangelism," *Prophetic Studies,* p. 33.
10. *The Truth,* Vol. IV, 1878, p. 452.

Chapter 4

The Believers' Meeting for Bible Study

1. Lewis Sperry Chafer, "Dispensationalism," *Bibliotheca Sacra,* Vol. XCIII, 1936, pp. 393-394.
2. The next four followed in 1886, 1895, 1914, 1918. There have been many since then, including one in New York in 1955.
3. E. P. Goodwin, "The Return of the Lord, Literal, Personal, Visible," *Prophetic Studies,* p. 7.
4. J. D. Herr, "Importance of Prophetic Study," *Prophetic Studies,* p. 152.
5. G. Campbell Morgan, *God's Methods With Man,* p. 57.
6. George S. Bishop, "Times of the Gentiles," *Prophetic Studies,* p. 50. (Italics mine.)
7. Henry Lummis, "Christ's Predictions," *Prophetic Studies,* p. 46.
8. S. H. Kellogg, "Premillennialism," *Bibliotheca Sacra,* Vol. XLV, 1888, p. 252.
9. Herr, *op. cit.,* p. 152.
10. Arno C. Gaebelein, *The History of the Scofield Reference Bible,* p. 31. Our Hope Publishing Co., 1943.
11. *The Truth,* Vol. V, 1879, p. 270.
12. *The Truth,* Vol. IV, 1878, pp. 450-451.
13. From the report of the meeting in *The Truth,* Vol. II, 1876, pp. 491 ff.
14. *Ibid.*
15. *The Truth,* Vol. III, 1877, p. 507.
16. From the report in *The Truth,* Vol. IV, 1878, p. 403.
17. Report for 1876, *loc. cit.*
18. *Ibid.* (Italics mine.) An archaic meaning of the word rapture is to transport. It is used by dispensationalists in this sense to distinguish between the two stages of Christ's second coming. In the rapture Christ is said to come *for* His saints. This coming allegedly takes place before the seven years of the Great Tribulation.
19. Report for 1877, *loc. cit.*

20. Report for 1878, *loc. cit.*
21. *The Truth,* Vol. IV, 1878, p. 452.

Chapter 5

The First International Prophecy Conferences

1. *The Truth,* Vol. V, 1879, p. 25.
2. Arno C. Gaebelein, *The History of the Scofield Reference Bible,* p. 32.
3. Nathaniel West, editor, *Premillennial Essays of the Prophetic Conference* (1878), p. 11.
4. *Ibid.,* p. 12.
5. *The New York Tribune* published the full proceedings of the conference, and printed an extra 50,000 copies for distribution.
6. *Premillennial Essays,* p. 8.
7. W. P. Mackay, "The Three Days' Feast with David's Son," *Premillennial Essays,* pp. 474-475.
8. *Ibid., et passim,* p. 474.
9. Rufus W. Clark, "Hope of Christ's Coming as a Motive to Holy Living and Active Labor," *Premillennial Essays,* p. 444.
10. See outline on pp. 31-32.
11. W. R. Nicholson, "The Gathering of Israel," *Premillennial Essays,* p. 236.
12. Chas. K. Imbrie, "The Regeneration," *Premillennial Essays,* p. 42.
13. *Premillennial Essays,* p. 149.
14. *Ibid.,* p. 115.
15. H. Lummis, "The Kingdom and the Church," *Premillennial Essays,* p. 189.
16. *Ibid.,* p. 195.
17. John T. Duffield, "A Summary of the Argument in Defence of Premillenarianism," *Premillennial Essays,* p. 406.
18. *Loc. cit.,* p. 256.
19. *The Truth,* Vol. XI, 1885, p. 413.
20. George Needham, editor, *Prophetic Studies of the International Prophetic Conference,* p. 5.
21. *Ibid.,* pp. 215-216.
22. W. E. Blackstone, "Missions," *Prophetic Studies,* p. 200.
23. *Ibid.*
24. A. T. Pierson, "Premillennial Motives to Evangelism," *Prophetic Studies,* p. 31.
25. *Ibid.,* p. 32.

26. George S. Bishop, "Times of the Gentiles," *Prophetic Studies*, p. 49.
27. W. R. Nicholson, "Messiah's Kingly Glory," *Prophetic Studies*, pp. 145-146.
28. W. R. Nicholson, "The Gathering of Israel," *Premillennial Essays*, p. 229.
29. *Prophetic Studies*, p. 138.
30. *Ibid.*, p. 140.
31. A. J. Gordon, "Spiritualism, Ritualism, Theosophy," *Prophetic Studies*, p. 63.
32. Maurice Baldwin, "The Power of This Truth to Stimulate the Work of Evangelization," *Prophetic Studies*, p. 210.
33. Gordon, *op. cit.*, p. 71.
34. John T. Duffield, "The Apostolic Church Was Premillenarian," *Prophetic Studies*, p. 181.
35. A. J. Frost, "Condition of the Church and World at Christ's Second Advent," *Prophetic Studies*, pp. 174, 177.
36. "Reasons for Holding the Bible and Prophetic Conference," *Prophetic Studies*, p. 216.

Chapter 6

The Decline of the Niagara Bible Conference

1. Arno C. Gaebelein, *The History of the Scofield Reference Bible*, p. 34.
2. Robert Cameron, *Scriptural Truth About the Lord's Return*, pp. 145-146. Fleming H. Revell, 1922. Used by permission.
3. Arno C. Gaebelein, *Half a Century*, pp. 153-154.
4. Robert Cameron, "Premillennialists," *The Watchword*, Vol. XIX, January, 1897, p. 3.
5. Cameron, *Scriptural Truth*, pp. 20, 148.
6. Nathaniel West, "The New Evangelism," *The Watchword*, Vol. XVIII, September, 1896, p. 246.
7. *Ibid.*
8. George Ricker Berry, *Premillennialism and Old Testament Prediction*, A Study in Interpretation, p. 12. University of Chicago Press, 1929.
9. *The Truth*, Vol. XXIII, 1897, p. 258.
10. Cameron had been coeditor of *The Watchword* during the last years of Gordon's life and continued the paper after his death. As early as 1895 he and Brookes talked over the possibility of merging their magazines, but the merger did not take place until after Brookes' death.

11. *The Watchword and Truth,* May, 1898, p. 145.
12. *Ibid.,* Vol. XXI, October and November issues.
13. *The Watchword and Truth,* Vol. XXII, July, 1900, p. 227.
14. *Ibid.,* Vol. XXII, December, 1900, p. 356.
15. See Gaebelein, *The History of the Scofield Reference Bible,* pp. 40-41.
16. James E. Bear, "Historic Premillennialism," *Union Seminary Review,* Vol. LV, May, 1944, p. 219.
17. See W. M. Horton, *Realistic Theology* (Part II of *Theology in Transition*), p. 15. Harper & Brothers, 1934.
18. A. T. Pierson, "Premillennial Motives to Evangelism," *Prophetic Studies,* p. 37.
19. W. E. Blackstone, "Missions," *Prophetic Studies,* p. 200.
20. *Ibid.,* p. 202.
21. A. J. Frost, "Conditions of the Church and World at Christ's Second Advent," *Prophetic Studies,* p. 174.
22. A. T. Pierson, "The Coming of the Lord," *The Truth,* Vol. XXII, 1896, pp. 634-635.
23. E. F. Stroeter, "Christ's Coming Pre-millennial," *Prophetic Studies,* pp. 19-20.
24. *Ibid.,* p. 19.
25. S. H. Kellogg, "Premillennialism," *Bibliotheca Sacra,* Vol. XLV, pp. 235-236.
26. *Ibid.,* p. 236.

Chapter 7
Scofield's Synthesis

1. Material for this biography is taken mostly from Arno C. Gaebelein, *The History of the Scofield Reference Bible,* pp. 18-27.
2. Mauro's statement that he first got his dispensationalism from Malachi Taylor is very unlikely, though they became acquainted later.
3. Gaebelein, *The History of the Scofield Reference Bible,* p. 22.
4. C. I. Scofield, "God's Purpose in This Age," *Our Hope,* Vol. VIII, March, 1902, pp. 465-466.
5. Quoted in Gaebelein, *The History of the Scofield Reference Bible,* p. 52.
6. Henry G. Weston, William J. Erdman, Arthur T. Pierson, W. G. Moorehead, Elmore Harris, Arno C. Gaebelein. William L. Pettingill's name was added to later editions.
7. It is very difficult to assess Gaebelein's real influence since I have

been limited mainly to an account by Gaebelein himself. However, it is clear that they were very close friends and shared viewpoints.

8. Ehlert says, "It would have to be assumed that the consulting editors of the *Scofield Reference Bible* endorsed the dispensational scheme and teachings of it and all that is thereby entailed. . . ." See "A Bibliography of Dispensationalism," *Bibliotheca Sacra*, Vol. CII, p. 457. Gaebelein says, however, that there was not full agreement in all the consultations made with the editors. *The History of the Scofield Reference Bible*, p. 59. As we have noted earlier, Erdman and Moorehead did not accept the pretribulation rapture or the "any-moment theory."

9. Arno C. Gaebelein, *Half a Century*, p. 85. (Italics mine.)

10. Alexander Reese, *The Approaching Advent*, p. 19.

11. C. I. Scofield, editor, *The Scofield Reference Bible*, p. 5. Oxford University Press, 1909. Used by permission.

12. Lewis Sperry Chafer, "Dispensationalism," *Bibliotheca Sacra*, Vol. XCIII, p. 391.

13. Arnold Ehlert, "A Bibliography of Dispensationalism," *Bibliotheca Sacra*, Vol. CII, p. 219. (Italics mine.)

14. William Kelly, *Lectures on Matthew*, p. 257. (Italics mine.) Loizeaux Brothers, 1943. (Reprint of 1868 edition.)

15. *The Scofield Reference Bible*, p. 16.

16. *Ibid.*, p. 20.

17. *Ibid.*, p. 1297.

18. *Ibid.*, p. 20.

19. *Ibid.*

20. *Ibid.* Scripture references are omitted.

21. *The Scofield Reference Bible*, p. 1115.

22. *Ibid.*

23. *Ibid.*, p. 1298.

24. *Ibid.*, p. 25.

25. *Ibid.*, p. 1250.

26. *Ibid.*, p. 1227.

27. Quoted by Roy L. Aldrich, "An Apologetic for Dispensationalism," *Bibliotheca Sacra*, Vol. CXII, pp. 50-51. Used by permission.

28. *Ibid.*, p. 51.

29. *The Scofield Reference Bible*, p. 1115.

30. *Ibid.*, p. 1002.

31. *Ibid.*, p. 6.

32. *Ibid.*, p. 16.

33. *Ibid.*, p. 250.

34. *Ibid.*, p. 20.

35. Lewis Sperry Chafer, *Systematic Theology*, Vol. I, p. 42. Dallas Seminary Press, 1948.

36. *The Scofield Reference Bible,* p. 1297.
37. C. I. Scofield, *Rightly Dividing the Word of Truth.* Loizeaux Brothers, Publishers (n.d.). The ten points listed are the ten chapters in the book.
38. *The Scofield Reference Bible,* p. 1151.
39. *Ibid.,* p. 1148.
40. *Ibid.,* p. 1000.
41. Chafer, *Systematic Theology,* Vol. IV, p. 12.
42. *The Scofield Reference Bible,* p. 1003.
43. *Ibid.,* p. 1150. Compare the fuller discussion in his *Plain Papers on the Doctrine of the Holy Spirit.*
44. C. I. Scofield, "God's Purpose in This Age," *Our Hope,* Vol. VIII, p. 465.
45. *The Scofield Reference Bible,* p. iii.
46. C. I. Scofield, *Plain Papers on the Doctrine of the Holy Spirit,* p. 29. Fleming H. Revell, 1899.
47. *Ibid.,* pp. 29-30. Compare also his footnotes on pp. 981 ff. and 1149 ff. in *The Scofield Reference Bible.*
48. Scofield, *Plain Papers on the Doctrine of the Holy Spirit,* pp. 31-32.
49. *Ibid.,* p. 34.
50. *The Scofield Reference Bible,* p. 1164.
51. Scofield, *Plain Papers on the Doctrine of the Holy Spirit,* p. 35.
52. *The Scofield Reference Bible,* p. 1021.
53. Kelly, *op. cit.,* p. 222.

Index